MONTENEGRO TRAVEL GUIDE 2024 AND BEYOND

A Complete Guide to Exploring Must-See Attractions, Enjoying Cultural Experiences, Indulging in Delicious Cuisine, and Making the Most of Your Adventure

By
ELLA NOMAD

Copyright 2024

All rights reserved

Montenegro MAP

SCAN THE QR CODE

Using an iPhone:
1. Open the Camera app on your iPhone.
2. Point the camera at the QR code. The camera will automatically scan the QR code.
3. A link will pop up above the code. Tap the link to open it

Using an Android phone:
1. Open the Camera app.
2. Tap the cog icon (usually in the top-left corner) to access the Camera settings.
3. Toggle on "Scan QR codes" or "Google Lens suggestions" (depending on your device).
4. Point the camera at the QR code, and a link will appear below the camera feed

Table of Contents

INTRODUCTION 5
   Crafting Your Montenegrin Adventure 10
Part 1: Unveiling Montenegro 15
   A Land of Dramatic Contrasts... 15
      Conquering the Peaks: Exploring Montenegro's National Parks 15
      Azure Paradise: Unveiling the Beauty of the Adriatic Coast (Budva, Kotor, Sveti Stefan) 28
      Lakes and Serenity 36
   Echoes of Empires: Exploring Medieval Towns................... 43
      Monuments and Museums 48
      Njegoš Mausoleum... 53
      Festivals and Traditions 57
      Grape Festival 62
Part 2: Embark on an Adventure 67
   Hitting the Trails: Hiking, Biking, and Outdoor Activities in Montenegro 67
      Hiking Adventures in Durmitor National Park 67
      Cycling Paradise: Exploring the Coast and Mountains on Two Wheels 72
      White-Water Rafting on the Tara River, Kayaking on Skadar Lake 77
Part 3: A Culinary Journey 82
   Fresh Flavors from Land and Sea 82
      Seafood Delights 82

   Savoring Local Specialties (Gulaš, Pršut, Kačamak) 87

   Montenegrin Pastries and Desserts 90

Part 4: Practical Planning 93

  Essential Information for Your Montenegrin Adventure ... 93

   Visas and Currency Exchange 93

   Getting There and Getting Around: Transportation Options in Montenegro 96

   Finding Your Perfect Accommodation: From Budget Hostels to Luxury Resorts 106

   Packing Essentials for All Seasons and Activities 112

  Montenegro Beyond 118

   Secret Beaches 118

   Charming Villages 120

   Bargaining at Local Markets and Shopping for Souvenirs 123

Conclusion 128

INTRODUCTION

Lay close like a hidden emerald between the dramatic peaks of the Dinaric Alps and the sparkling turquoise waters of the Adriatic Sea, lies Montenegro – a country that packs a mighty punch despite its diminutive size. Often overshadowed by its Balkan neighbors, Montenegro unveils itself to the adventurous traveler as a land of breathtaking beauty, rich history, and soul-stirring experiences.

Imagine yourself standing on the ramparts of Kotor's medieval old town, the sun-drenched stone buildings cascading down to a calm harbor where sleek yachts bob gently. The echoes of Venetian rule linger in the labyrinthine streets, while the distant peaks of Lovćen National Park pierce the azure sky. This is just a taste of the captivating drape that is Montenegro.

A Land Steeped in History

Montenegro's past is as dramatic and exhilarating as its landscapes. From the early settlements of the Illyrians to the Roman conquest and subsequent Byzantine rule, the land has been a crossroads of empires. The 14th century marked the rise of the powerful Crnojević dynasty, who established the first Montenegrin state and fiercely defended their independence against the Ottomans. This period laid the foundation for the country's strong national identity, where resilience and a spirit of defiance became deeply ingrained.

The 19th century witnessed the reign of Prince Nikola I Petrović-Njegoš, a visionary leader who ushered in a golden age of modernization and reform. Montenegro finally secured its independence from Ottoman rule in the epic Battle of Mojkovac in 1876, a pivotal moment that cemented the country's place on the map. The tumultuous 20th century saw Montenegro embroiled in the Balkan Wars and World Wars, eventually becoming a part of Yugoslavia. However, the yearning for self-determination remained strong, culminating in Montenegro's peaceful separation from Serbia in 2006.

A Paradise for Adventure Seekers

Montenegro is a playground for those with an insatiable thirst for adventure. Hike through the pristine wilderness of Durmitor National Park, scaling the majestic Bobotov Kuk, the highest peak in the country, and be rewarded with panoramic vistas that stretch for miles. Embark on a white-water rafting expedition down the Tara River, navigating through thrilling rapids and emerald canyons carved by millennia of rushing water. Kayak across the serene expanse of Skadar Lake, Europe's largest freshwater lake, a haven for diverse birdlife and a UNESCO World Natural Heritage Site.

For the adrenaline junkies, zipline across the breathtaking Bay of Kotor, feeling the wind rush through your hair as you soar above the turquoise waters. Explore the Lipa Cave system, one of the largest underground complexes in Europe, marveling at the intricate speleothems and hidden chambers. For a different perspective, saddle up and explore the rolling hills and dramatic valleys of the highlands on horseback, experiencing the timeless beauty of Montenegro's rural landscapes.

A Culinary Journey for the Senses

Montenegro's cuisine is a symphony of fresh, seasonal flavors influenced by its rich history and diverse geography. Indulge in the bounty of the Adriatic Sea with succulent seafood dishes like "brodet" – a fisherman's stew bursting with flavor, or "mušle na buzaru" – plump mussels cooked in white wine and garlic sauce. Venture inland and savor the hearty stews and casseroles that are the soul of Montenegrin cuisine. "Gulaš," a rich beef stew with paprika and vegetables, is a national favorite, while "kačamak," a creamy polenta dish, is a comforting staple. Don't miss out on "pršut," air-dried ham cured in the fresh mountain air, a delicacy best enjoyed with a glass of local wine.

For a taste of tradition, head to a cozy "konoba," a family-run tavern, and experience the warmth of Montenegrin hospitality. Savor local specialties alongside homemade rakia, a potent Balkan brandy, and engage in lively conversation with locals. End your meal with a decadent serving of "baklava," a flaky pastry layered with nuts and drenched in honey, or "krepschta," a layered filo pastry dessert filled with sweet or savory fillings.

Beyond the Tourist Trail

Montenegro offers a wealth of experiences that lie beyond the well-trodden tourist path. Discover the charming village of Njeguši, lay close in the foothills of Lovćen National Park, the birthplace of Peter the Great, a ruler who modernized Montenegro and left a lasting legacy. Explore the serene beauty of Skadar Lake, a haven for birdwatchers, where traditional fishing villages dot the shoreline and time seems to slow down. Venture off the beaten track and discover hidden coves accessible only by boat, where crystal-clear waters lap against pristine beaches and the sound of the waves provides a natural soundtrack to your relaxation.

Montenegro is a land of contrasts, where rugged mountains meet the sparkling Adriatic and ancient history intertwines with a vibrant contemporary culture. Here, time seems to bend, allowing you to experience the serenity of centuries-old monasteries lay close amidst dramatic landscapes, followed by the pulsating nightlife of coastal towns like Budva and Tivat. Whether you seek a tranquil escape or an action-packed adventure, Montenegro caters to every traveler's desire.

Unveiling a Balkan Paradise

As you embark on your Montenegrin adventure, prepare to be captivated by the warmth and hospitality of its people. A genuine smile and a friendly greeting are the norm here, and locals take pride in sharing their beloved country with visitors. Immerse yourself in the vibrant culture, where ancient traditions live on through lively folk festivals, captivating music, and intricate handicrafts. Witness the annual Kotor Carnival, a riotous celebration with flamboyant costumes, elaborate parades, and a contagious energy that will leave you exhilarated. In the charming village of Perast, take a boat trip to visit the picturesque islands of Our Lady of the Rocks and St. George, where centuries-old churches stand sentinel over the calm waters of the bay.

A Haven for Nature Lovers

Montenegro's natural beauty is truly awe-inspiring. Explore the dramatic landscapes of Biogradska Gora National Park, a haven for pristine forests, serene glacial lakes, and a rich diversity of flora and fauna. Hike through verdant valleys carpeted with wildflowers, or simply relax by the shores of Black Lake, a jewel lay close amidst the mountains, and soak in the tranquility. For a touch of luxury, indulge in a stay at one of the charming eco-lodges lay close within national parks, where sustainable practices blend seamlessly with modern amenities, allowing you to experience the wonders of nature without compromising on comfort.

Planning Your Dream Montenegrin Adventure

This guide serves as your indispensable companion as you navigate the wonders of Montenegro. Whether you're a seasoned traveler or embarking on your first international adventure, we've compiled essential information to ensure a smooth and unforgettable experience. From obtaining the necessary visas and navigating the local currency to choosing the perfect mode of transportation and finding comfortable accommodation, we've got you covered. We'll equip you with insider tips on finding the best deals, bargaining at local markets, and avoiding tourist traps.

This guide delves deeper than just the must-see sights, offering cultural insights and practical advice to help you connect with the local people, traditions, and customs. By learning a few basic Montenegrin phrases, you'll open doors to richer interactions and a deeper appreciation of the country's soul. We've also included a curated list of recommended reading materials and resources to further fuel your wanderlust and allow you to delve deeper into Montenegro's rich history and captivating culture.

A Journey Awaits

Montenegro is a destination that stays with you long after you've returned home. It's a place where the dramatic beauty of nature leaves you breathless, the rich history whispers stories in your ear, and the warmth of the people touches your heart. This guide is your invitation to embark on an unforgettable journey through this

Balkan paradise. So, pack your bags, embrace the spirit of adventure, and prepare to be enchanted by the magic of Montenegro.

Crafting Your Montenegrin Adventure

"The world is a book, and those who do not travel read only a page," penned Saint Augustine, a sentiment that perfectly encapsulates the transformative power of exploration. Montenegro, with its diverse landscapes, rich history, and vibrant culture, promises to be a captivating chapter in your travelogue. This chapter serves as your compass, guiding you in crafting the perfect Montenegrin itinerary – one that caters to your interests, travel style, and desired pace.

Tailoring Your Adventure

The beauty of Montenegro lies in its ability to cater to a broad spectrum of travelers. Are you a history buff yearning to delve into the country's rich past? An adrenaline junkie seeking heart-pounding adventures? Or perhaps a gourmand eager to savor the delectable flavors of Montenegrin cuisine? No matter your preference, Montenegro has something to offer.

The History Buff's Itinerary

Immerse yourself in Montenegro's fascinating past by embarking on a journey through time. Start your exploration in the UNESCO-listed old town of Kotor, where Venetian architecture whispers tales of a bygone era. Wander through the labyrinthine streets, marveling at the imposing city walls and the majestic Cathedral of Saint Tryphon. Climb the ramparts of the fortress and be rewarded with breathtaking panoramic views of the Bay of Kotor.

Next, journey to Cetinje, the former royal capital, boasting an array of museums and historical landmarks. Explore the National Museum of Montenegro, housing artifacts that illuminate the country's vibrant history. Pay your respects at the mausoleum of Petar II Petrović-Njegoš, a towering structure perched atop Mount Lovćen, offering stunning vistas of the surrounding landscapes.

Don't miss the chance to visit the historic town of Perast, lay close on the shores of the Bay of Kotor. Here, time seems to stand still as you stroll past baroque palaces and charming churches. Take a boat trip to visit the picturesque islands of Our Lady of the Rocks and St. George, where centuries-old monasteries stand sentinel over the calm waters.

The Adventure Seeker's Itinerary

For those with an insatiable thirst for adrenaline, Montenegro offers a plethora of thrilling experiences. Lace up your hiking boots and conquer the majestic peaks of Durmitor National Park. Scale Bobotov Kuk, the highest peak in Montenegro, and be rewarded with unparalleled panoramic views. Embark on a white-water rafting adventure down the Tara River, navigating through exhilarating rapids and emerald canyons.

For a different perspective, soar above the breathtaking Bay of Kotor on a zipline, feeling the wind rush through your hair as you experience the dramatic landscapes from a bird's-eye view. Explore the wonders hidden beneath the surface by venturing into the Lipa Cave system, one of the largest underground complexes in Europe. Marvel at the intricate speleothems and hidden chambers as you journey through this subterranean wonderland.

The Foodie's Itinerary

Montenegro is a paradise for gourmands, offering a symphony of fresh, seasonal flavors influenced by its rich history and diverse geography. Indulge in the bounty of the Adriatic Sea with succulent seafood dishes like "brodet," a fisherman's stew bursting with flavor, or "mušle na buzaru," plump mussels cooked in white wine and garlic sauce.

Venture inland and delve into the world of hearty stews and casseroles that are the soul of Montenegrin cuisine. Sample "gulaš," a rich beef stew with paprika and vegetables, a national favorite, or savor "kačamak," a creamy polenta dish, a comforting staple. Don't miss out on "pršut," air-dried ham cured in the fresh mountain air, a delicacy best enjoyed with a glass of local wine.

For a truly immersive experience, head to a cozy "konoba," a family-run tavern, and experience the warmth of Montenegrin hospitality. Savor local specialties alongside homemade rakia, a potent Balkan brandy, and engage in lively conversation with locals. End your meal with a decadent serving of "baklava," a flaky pastry layered with nuts and drenched in honey, or "krepschta," a layered filo pastry dessert filled with sweet or savory fillings.

Crafting Your Ideal Itinerary

With so much to see and do, crafting the perfect Montenegrin itinerary can feel overwhelming. However, this guide is here to help. Consider the length of your trip and prioritize the experiences that resonate most with you. For a week-long adventure, you could base yourself in coastal towns like Budva or Kotor, venturing out on day trips to explore historical sites, national parks, and charming villages. If you have two weeks or more, consider venturing further inland, exploring the dramatic landscapes of the north and indulging in a slower pace of life.

Mixing and Matching

The beauty of Montenegro lies in its ability to seamlessly blend different experiences. For instance, after a thrilling hike through Durmitor National Park, you could unwind on the pristine beaches of Sveti Stefan, soaking up the sun and indulging in water sports.

Alternatively, balance your exploration of historical sites like the Njegoš Mausoleum with a visit to a local winery, savoring award-winning Montenegrin wines amidst breathtaking scenery.

Festivals and Events

To truly immerse yourself in the vibrant culture of Montenegro, consider planning your trip around a local festival or event. Join the revelry of the Kotor Carnival, a riotous celebration with flamboyant costumes, elaborate parades, and a contagious energy that will leave you exhilarated. In the charming village of Perast, witness the annual Fašinada, a traditional boat procession commemorating the sinking of a Venetian ship. For music lovers, the Budva Theatre City Festival offers a vibrant celebration of performing arts, held against the backdrop of the historic old town.

Finding Your Pace

Montenegro caters to all travel styles. If you're a fast-paced traveler who thrives on ticking off landmarks, you can pack your itinerary with exciting activities and day trips. However, Montenegro also rewards those who slow down and savor the moment. Spend a lazy afternoon sipping strong Montenegrin coffee in a sun-drenched piazza, people-watching and soaking in the atmosphere. Opt for a stay in a charming guesthouse lay close in a rural village, allowing yourself to truly connect with the local way of life.

Respecting Local Customs

As you embark on your Montenegrin adventure, remember to be a respectful guest. Dress modestly when visiting religious sites, and be mindful of noise levels in quiet areas. While tipping is not customary in Montenegro, a small gratuity for exceptional service is always appreciated. Learning a few basic Montenegrin phrases will go a long way in establishing rapport with locals and enriching your experience.

Embrace the Unexpected

The beauty of travel lies in the unexpected encounters and experiences that leave a lasting impression. Don't be afraid to veer off the beaten path and explore hidden gems. Strike up conversations with locals, who will be more than happy to share their insider tips and stories. Embrace the spontaneity that comes with travel, and allow Montenegro to surprise and delight you in unexpected ways.

With careful planning and an open mind, you can craft the perfect Montenegrin itinerary, one that caters to your interests and desires. This guide serves as your starting point, but ultimately, the most rewarding experiences will be the ones you discover along the way. So, pack your bags, embrace the spirit of adventure, and get ready to create unforgettable memories in the heart of the Balkans.

Part 1: Unveiling Montenegro
A LAND OF DRAMATIC CONTRASTS

Conquering the Peaks: Exploring Montenegro's National Parks

The dramatic peaks of Montenegro's national parks beckon to adventurous souls, promising breathtaking vistas, invigorating challenges, and an intimate connection with nature. Among these crown jewels, Durmitor National Park stands out as a true hiker's paradise, a land sculpted by glaciers where jagged peaks pierce the azure sky and emerald valleys cradle pristine lakes. Lace up your boots and prepare to embark on a challenging yet rewarding hike to Bobotov Kuk, the highest peak in Montenegro, a journey that will test your physical limits and leave you breathless in more ways than one.

A Dawn Ascent

Your adventure begins before the first rays of dawn paint the sky. Emerging from your cozy guesthouse in the charming town of Žabljak, a gateway to Durmitor National Park, a crisp mountain air invigorates your senses. Headlamps illuminate the path as you embark on the well-marked trail leading towards Crno Jezero (Black Lake), a tranquil glacial lake reflecting the star-studded night sky. The air is still, broken only by the rhythmic crunch of your boots on the gravel path and the occasional hooting of an owl perched in a nearby pine tree.

As the first blush of dawn paints the eastern horizon, casting a soft glow on the surrounding peaks, you reach Crno Jezero. The still waters mirror the awakening landscape, creating a scene of ethereal beauty. Take a moment to savor the tranquility, to breathe in the crisp mountain air, and to fuel your body for the challenging journey ahead.

The Ascent Begins

The trail leading up Bobotov Kuk is a steady climb, gaining elevation with each step. The initial section winds through a dense forest, a canopy of towering pines and lush greenery providing welcome shade from the sun that begins to rise higher in the sky. Keep an eye out for the diverse flora that thrives in Durmitor. Spot delicate alpine flowers clinging to rocky outcrops, their vibrant colors contrasting with the rugged landscape. Listen for the melodic calls of birds flitting through the branches, a symphony of nature that accompanies your ascent.

As you emerge from the forest, the landscape transforms dramatically. Rugged, rocky terrain unfolds before you, demanding a more deliberate pace and a sure footing. The air thins slightly, and a cool breeze whips through your hair, carrying the invigorating scent of pine and wild herbs. Here, the scale of Durmitor National Park becomes truly evident. Jagged peaks pierce the sky in every direction, their snow-capped summits glistening in the morning sun. Emerald valleys carve through the landscape, dotted with glacial lakes that resemble scattered sapphires.

Reaching for the Summit

The final push to Bobotov Kuk requires a degree of physical fitness and a healthy dose of determination. The trail becomes steeper, with sections involving scrambling over loose rock and navigating narrow ridges. However, the reward for your perseverance is truly magnificent. With each step, the panoramic views become more breathtaking. The sprawling valleys of Durmitor unfold beneath you, a drape of green and blue, dotted with villages that resemble miniature toy towns. On a clear day, your gaze may even reach the sparkling Adriatic Sea, a shimmering ribbon on the horizon.

The World at Your Feet

Finally, after hours of challenging yet exhilarating ascent, you reach the summit of Bobotov Kuk. A sense of accomplishment washes over you as you stand at the highest point in Montenegro, the world seemingly stretched out at your feet. Take a deep breath and savor the panoramic vista that stretches in all directions. Feel the wind whipping through your hair and the warmth of the sun on your skin. This is a moment etched in memory, a testament to your physical prowess and a reminder of the awe-inspiring beauty of nature.

A Descent Filled with Wonder

The descent from Bobotov Kuk is a different kind of adventure. Your legs may feel tired, but the sense of accomplishment fuels your steps. The landscape takes on a new perspective as you descend, revealing hidden crevices and secluded valleys that were invisible from the summit. Keep an eye out for the unique fauna that calls Durmitor National Park home. Spot nimble chamois goats gracefully navigating the rocky slopes, or marmots sunning themselves on boulders, their shrill whistles echoing through the mountains.

A Well-Earned Reward

As you reach the base of the mountain, a wave of relief washes over you, tinged with a deep sense of satisfaction. The challenging climb has pushed you to your limits, but the rewards are immeasurable. You've conquered one of Montenegro's most iconic peaks, witnessed breathtaking vistas, and connected with the raw beauty of nature.

Beyond the Climb

While the ascent of Bobotov Kuk is an unforgettable experience, Durmitor National Park offers a plethora of hiking trails for all skill levels. Explore the serene beauty of glacial lakes like Zabojsko

Jezero and Veliko Škrcko Jezero, their crystal-clear waters reflecting the surrounding peaks. Embark on a shorter trek through the Black Lake Cirque, a glacial valley dotted with wildflowers and offering panoramic views of the surrounding landscape. For a truly unique perspective, venture into the depths of the Ice Cave, a natural wonder where subterranean chambers are adorned with glistening ice formations.

Beyond Durmitor

Montenegro's drape of national parks extends beyond the majestic peaks of Durmitor. Hike through the verdant forests of Biogradska Gora National Park, a haven for ancient trees, diverse wildlife, and serene glacial lakes. Explore the dramatic landscapes of Prokletije National Park, a hiker's paradise with soaring peaks, deep canyons, and hidden glacial lakes. Kayak across the expansive waters of Skadar Lake National Park, a haven for birdwatchers, and explore the charming fishing villages that dot the shoreline.

Respecting the Mountain

Hiking in Montenegro's national parks is an exhilarating experience, but it's crucial to prioritize safety and respect the fragile ecosystem. Always check weather conditions before setting off and choose a trail that matches your skill level and physical fitness. Wear appropriate clothing and footwear, and be sure to pack enough water and snacks for your journey. Leave no trace behind, by disposing of waste properly and minimizing your impact on the environment.

A Journey of Self-Discovery

Hiking in the mountains of Montenegro is more than just a physical challenge; it's a journey of self-discovery. As you push your limits and conquer challenging climbs, you develop a sense of resilience and inner strength. The breathtaking views and the serenity of nature provide an opportunity to disconnect from the everyday hustle and bustle and reconnect with yourself. You may find yourself reflecting on life's bigger questions, appreciating the simple beauty of the moment, and returning home with a renewed sense of perspective.

Memories Etched in Stone

Your adventures in Montenegro's national parks will leave a lasting impression. The memories of conquering challenging climbs, witnessing breathtaking vistas, and connecting with the raw beauty of nature will stay with you long after you return home. These experiences will serve as a constant reminder of your strength, your spirit of adventure, and the awe-inspiring power of the natural world. So, lace up your boots, embrace the challenge, and get ready to discover the magic of Montenegro's national parks.

Tackling Montenegro's Trails: A Hiker's Guide

The dramatic landscapes of Montenegro's national parks are a haven for outdoor enthusiasts, offering a diverse range of hiking trails catering to all skill levels. Whether you're a seasoned mountaineer seeking a challenging ascent or a casual explorer looking for a scenic stroll, Montenegro's trails promise breathtaking vistas, invigorating exercise, and an intimate connection with nature. This chapter equips you with the essential information to tackle various hiking trails, ensuring a safe and rewarding experience.

Deciphering the Difficulty Levels

Montenegro's hiking trails are categorized by difficulty levels, allowing you to choose a path that matches your experience and fitness level. Here's a breakdown of the common difficulty classifications:

- **Easy:** These trails are generally well-maintained and suitable for families with children or those seeking a leisurely stroll. They involve minimal elevation gain and offer mostly flat or gentle inclines.

- **Moderate:** Moderate trails offer a slightly greater challenge with moderate elevation gain and some uneven terrain. They may involve sections with loose rocks or steps, requiring a moderate level of fitness.

- **Difficult:** Difficult trails are designed for experienced hikers and require a good level of fitness and stamina. They involve significant elevation gain, steep inclines, and potentially challenging terrain like scree slopes or exposed sections.

- **Expert:** Expert trails are only recommended for highly experienced and well-equipped hikers. These trails involve extreme challenges, including technical sections, significant elevation gain, and potentially dangerous terrain.

Choosing Your Trail

With a wide variety of trails at your disposal, choosing the right one can feel overwhelming. Here are some factors to consider:

- **Your Fitness Level:** Be honest about your physical capabilities and choose a trail that matches your current fitness level. Don't overestimate your abilities, especially when tackling challenging hikes in high-altitude environments.

- **Time Available:** Consider the length of your hike and allocate enough time to complete it comfortably. Factor in rest breaks, photo opportunities, and potential delays due to weather or unforeseen circumstances.

- **Interest Level:** Do you crave breathtaking summits or prefer a scenic walk through a valley? Choose a trail that aligns with your interests, whether it's reaching a mountain peak, exploring a glacial lake, or simply enjoying a stroll through a verdant forest.

- **Travel Style:** Are you a solo adventurer or traveling with a group? Some trails may be more suitable for solo exploration, while others might be best enjoyed with companions.

Essential Gear

Packing the right gear is crucial for a safe and enjoyable hike. The specific equipment you need will depend on the difficulty of the trail, the time of year, and the weather conditions. Here's a list of essential items for most hikes in Montenegro:

- **Durable Hiking Boots:** Invest in a good pair of sturdy and comfortable hiking boots that provide ankle support and good traction on uneven terrain.
- **Weather-Appropriate Clothing:** Pack layers of clothing that you can adjust depending on weather changes. A base layer for moisture management, a mid-layer for insulation, and a waterproof outer layer are essential.
- **Sun Protection:** Pack a hat with a brim, sunglasses with UV protection, and sunscreen with a high SPF to shield yourself from the sun's rays.
- **Navigation Tools:** A map and compass or a GPS device are crucial for navigating trails, especially in remote areas. Download offline maps and familiarize yourself with the route before setting off.
- **Hydration Pack:** Stay hydrated throughout your hike by carrying a refillable water bottle or a hydration pack with enough water for the duration of your journey.
- **Snacks and Lunch:** Pack high-energy snacks like nuts, dried fruit, and granola bars to keep your energy levels up during the hike. Pack a nutritious lunch for longer hikes.

- **First-Aid Kit:** Be prepared for minor injuries by carrying a basic first-aid kit containing essential supplies like bandages, antiseptic wipes, and pain medication.
- **Headlamp or Flashlight:** If you plan to hike during dawn or dusk, pack a headlamp or flashlight with extra batteries to illuminate your path.
- **Waste Disposal Bag:** Respect the environment by packing a small bag to dispose of any waste you generate during your hike.

Trailblazer's Toolkit

Now that you're armed with the essential information, let's delve into some specific trails within Montenegro's captivating national parks:

Durmitor National Park

- **Bobotov Kuk (Difficult, 8-10 hours):** The crown jewel of Montenegrin hiking, conquering Bobotov Kuk, the highest peak in the country, is a challenging yet rewarding experience. The trail involves a steep ascent with significant elevation gain, requiring a high level of fitness and potentially technical sections. Prepare for a long day with breathtaking panoramic views at the summit.
- **Essential Gear:** Sturdy hiking boots, trekking poles (optional but helpful), warm layers (temperatures can drop significantly at higher altitudes), headlamp for early starts or late descents, and a good supply of water and high-energy snacks.
- **Crno Jezero Loop (Easy, 2-3 hours):** This scenic trail encircles the tranquil Black Lake, offering stunning views of the surrounding mountains and a gentle introduction to the beauty of Durmitor National Park. The well-maintained path

is suitable for all fitness levels and a perfect option for families with children. **Essential Gear:** Comfortable walking shoes, sunscreen, hat, and water bottle.

- **Zabojsko Jezero Hike (Moderate, 4-5 hours):** This moderately challenging trail leads you to the pristine Zabojsko Jezero, a glacial lake lay close amidst dramatic mountain scenery. The path involves some climbs and uneven terrain, requiring a moderate level of fitness. The reward? A refreshing swim in the cool waters of the lake and breathtaking views of the surrounding peaks. **Essential Gear:** Hiking boots, backpack with water and snacks, swimsuit and towel (optional).

- **Ice Cave Trail (Moderate, 3-4 hours):** This unique trail leads you to the entrance of the Ice Cave, a natural wonder where subterranean chambers are adorned with glistening ice formations. The path involves some inclines and uneven terrain, with sections potentially icy in the early spring or late fall. **Essential Gear:** Hiking boots with good traction, warm layers (the cave can be chilly), headlamp for exploring the cave, and a sense of adventure.

Biogradska Gora National Park

- **Biogradska Lake Loop (Easy, 2-3 hours):** This easy trail circumnavigates the serene Biogradska Lake, a haven for diverse birdlife and surrounded by ancient forests. The well-maintained path is perfect for a leisurely stroll, allowing you to soak in the tranquility of the park. **Essential Gear:** Comfortable walking shoes, insect repellent (optional), camera to capture the scenery.

- **Jelova Stijena Viewpoint (Moderate, 3-4 hours):** This moderately challenging trail rewards you with panoramic vistas of Biogradska Gora National Park from the Jelova

Stijena viewpoint. The path involves some steeper sections and uneven terrain, requiring a moderate level of fitness. **Essential Gear:** Hiking boots, backpack with water and snacks, camera for capturing the breathtaking views.

- **Visitors Center to Black Lake (Moderate, 4-5 hours):** This scenic trail connects the park's Visitor Center with Black Lake, a jewel lay close amidst a dense forest. The path offers diverse landscapes, from lush forests to glacial meadows, and requires a moderate level of fitness for the climbs involved. **Essential Gear:** Hiking boots, backpack with water and snacks, insect repellent (optional).

Prokletije National Park

- **Hridski Krš - Visitor Center Loop (Moderate, 4-5 hours):** This loop trail takes you through the heart of Prokletije National Park, offering stunning views of the dramatic mountain peaks and lush valleys. The path involves some inclines and uneven terrain, with sections potentially muddy after rainfall. **Essential Gear:** Hiking boots with good traction, rain gear (depending on the forecast), backpack with water and snacks, camera to capture the scenery.

- **Hajla Prokletije (Difficult, 6-8 hours):** This challenging trail leads you to Hajla Prokletije, a high mountain plateau offering breathtaking panoramic views and a true wilderness experience. The path involves significant elevation gain, steep inclines, and potentially technical sections requiring a high level of fitness and experience. **Essential Gear:** Sturdy hiking boots, trekking poles (highly recommended), backpack with plenty of water and high-energy snacks, warm layers (temperatures can drop significantly at higher altitudes), headlamp for early starts or late descents, and a sense of adventure.

- **Grebaja Valley Hike (Moderate, 3-4 hours):** This scenic trail meanders through the picturesque Grebaja Valley, a haven for diverse flora and fauna. The path is well-maintained and offers stunning views of the surrounding mountains, with sections requiring moderate levels of fitness for the climbs. **Essential Gear:** Hiking boots, backpack with water and snacks, insect repellent (optional), camera to capture the scenery.

Safety First

Hiking in Montenegro's national parks is a rewarding experience, but safety should always be your top priority. Here are some essential safety tips to keep in mind:

- **Inform Someone of Your Plans:** Before setting off on any hike, let someone know your planned route, estimated time of return, and any potential risks involved.
- Check the Weather Forecast: Always check the weather forecast before venturing out on a hike. Be aware of potential thunderstorms, sudden changes in temperature, or heavy snowfall, and adjust your plans accordingly. Don't attempt challenging hikes in adverse weather conditions.
- **Stay Hydrated:** Dehydration is a serious risk, especially during strenuous hikes in hot weather. Carry enough water for the duration of your journey and replenish your fluids regularly.
- **Pack for the Unexpected:** Even on short hikes, it's wise to pack an emergency blanket, rain gear, and basic first-aid supplies. Unexpected weather changes or minor injuries can be mitigated with a little preparation.

- **Be Aware of Your Surroundings:** Keep an eye out for loose rocks, slippery sections, and potential hazards on the trail. Be mindful of wildlife encounters, especially in remote areas. Give way to descending hikers and maintain a safe distance from wildlife.
- **Respect the Environment:** Leave no trace behind by disposing of waste properly and minimizing your impact on the delicate ecosystems within the national parks. Stick to designated trails and avoid disturbing the flora and fauna.
- **Know Your Limits:** Don't push yourself beyond your physical capabilities. Turn back if you feel tired, unwell, or encounter unforeseen challenges. There's no shame in prioritizing safety and enjoying a shorter hike.
- **Embrace the Journey:** Montenegro's hiking trails offer more than just breathtaking views; they are an opportunity to connect with nature, challenge yourself, and experience a sense of accomplishment. Hike at your own pace, savor the moment, and disconnect from the everyday hustle and bustle.

Beyond the Trails

Hiking is just one way to experience the magic of Montenegro's national parks. For those seeking a more relaxed adventure, consider these options:

- **Scenic Drives:** Several national parks offer scenic drives that allow you to witness the dramatic landscapes from the comfort of your car. Cruise along winding roads and stop at designated viewpoints to capture breathtaking photos.
- **Mountain Biking:** For adrenaline seekers, explore designated mountain biking trails that wind through forests

and valleys, offering stunning views and a challenging workout.

- **Horseback Riding:** Embark on a unique adventure by exploring the national parks on horseback. This is a fantastic way to experience the beauty of the landscape from a different perspective, especially for those with limited mobility.

- **Wildlife Watching:** Montenegro's national parks are home to diverse wildlife, including bears, wolves, chamois, and a variety of birdlife. Join a guided tour or hike quietly through designated areas to potentially spot these magnificent creatures in their natural habitat.

Montenegro's national parks offer a drape of landscapes, from soaring peaks and pristine lakes to verdant forests and dramatic canyons. With a variety of hiking trails catering to all skill levels, the opportunity to explore these natural wonders awaits. So, lace up your boots, pack your essentials, and embark on an unforgettable adventure in the heart of the Balkans. Whether you conquer a challenging summit, meander through a scenic valley, or simply soak in the tranquility of nature, Montenegro's national parks promise an experience that will leave a lasting impression.

Azure Paradise: Unveiling the Beauty of the Adriatic Coast (Budva, Kotor, Sveti Stefan)

Montenegro's allure extends far beyond the dramatic peaks of its national parks. Kissing the shores of the Adriatic Sea lies a captivating coastline, an alluring drape of sun-drenched beaches, charming coastal towns, and dramatic cliffside settlements. This chapter invites you to delve into the azure paradise of Montenegro's Adriatic coast, where turquoise waters lap at golden shores, and medieval history whispers from ancient stone walls.

Budva: A Buzzing Seaside Gem

Budva, a vibrant coastal town, pulsates with energy. Its historic old town, a UNESCO World Heritage Site, is a labyrinth of narrow cobbled streets lined with Venetian-influenced architecture. Wander past terracotta-roofed houses adorned with colorful flower boxes, and marvel at the imposing city walls, silent sentinels guarding the town's rich past. Climb the ramparts of the Citadel for panoramic views of the shimmering Adriatic and the dramatic sweep of the coastline.

Beyond the old town, Budva transforms into a modern resort town. Sleek hotels line the pristine beaches, offering luxurious accommodations and a plethora of water sports activities. Indulge in sunbathing on the golden sands, or test your adrenaline on jet skis or kayaks, feeling the cool spray of the Adriatic on your skin. For the adventurous, explore hidden coves and secluded beaches accessible only by boat, where turquoise waters invite refreshing dips and pristine shores beckon for relaxation.

As the sun dips below the horizon, Budva transforms into a vibrant hub of nightlife. Stylish restaurants with open-air terraces tempt you with delectable seafood dishes and panoramic views. Lively bars pulsate with infectious energy, enticing you to linger over cocktails and soak in the electrifying atmosphere. Budva offers something for everyone, whether you crave a relaxing beach getaway or a vibrant nightlife scene.

Kotor: A Journey Through Time

Lay close at the end of the dramatic Bay of Kotor, a fjord-like inlet carved by glaciers, lies the enchanting town of Kotor. Enclosed by imposing medieval walls, Kotor is a UNESCO-listed treasure trove of history and architectural gems. Step inside the town's Old Town and embark on a journey through time. Stroll through narrow alleys lined with Baroque palaces, each one a testament to the town's rich Venetian heritage.

Climb the imposing city walls, a network of defensive fortifications that snake their way up the mountainside. The panoramic views from the ramparts are simply breathtaking, showcasing the turquoise waters of the bay, the charming town lay close below, and the dramatic peaks of Lovćen National Park in the distance. Visit the magnificent Cathedral of Saint Tryphon, a Romanesque masterpiece, and marvel at its intricate stonework and sacred treasures.

Beyond the historical treasures, Kotor offers a charming atmosphere. Peruse local shops overflowing with handcrafted souvenirs, from delicate lacework to intricate filigree jewelry. Savor a leisurely lunch in a sun-drenched piazza, people-watching and soaking in the relaxed pace of life. In the evenings, intimate restaurants tucked away in hidden courtyards serve delicious Montenegrin cuisine, accompanied by local wines and lively conversation.

Sveti Stefan: A Secluded Paradise

A short distance from Budva lies Sveti Stefan, a captivating islet transformed into a luxurious resort. Connected to the mainland by a narrow causeway, Sveti Stefan resembles a fairytale island, a cluster of terracotta-roofed houses cascading down a rocky outcrop and lapped by turquoise waters. While access to the islet itself is restricted to resort guests, you can still admire its beauty from afar.

Relax on the public beach adjacent to Sveti Stefan, bask in the warm Mediterranean sun, and soak in the stunning views. For a unique perspective, rent a kayak or paddleboard and explore the island's coastline, marveling at its beauty from a different vantage point. Indulge in a seafood feast at a beachfront restaurant, savoring fresh Adriatic catches while the gentle waves lap at the shore. Sveti Stefan, even from a distance, offers a glimpse into a world of luxury and serenity, a secluded paradise beckoning with its undeniable charm.

Beyond the Shores

The beauty of Montenegro's Adriatic coast extends beyond its iconic towns. Venture out and discover hidden gems:

- **Lustica Peninsula:** Explore the rugged beauty of the Lustica Peninsula, a haven for secluded beaches, charming villages, and dramatic cliffs overlooking the turquoise waters.

- **Petrovac:** Relax on the pristine beaches of Petrovac, a charming seaside town with a relaxed atmosphere and a picturesque harbor.

- **Njeguši:** Lay close in the foothills of Lovćen National Park lies Njeguši, a historic village offering breathtaking mountain views and a glimpse into traditional Montenegrin life.

Activities for Every Explorer

The Adriatic coast caters to all types of travelers, offering a plethora of activities beyond sunbathing and sightseeing. Here's a taste of what awaits:

- **Water Sports:** Embrace your inner adrenaline junkie with a variety of water sports. Test your skills on jet skis or kayaks, explore hidden coves on a stand-up paddleboard, or soar above the waves with parasailing. For a more tranquil experience, try snorkeling or diving and discover the vibrant underwater world teeming with colorful fish and fascinating marine life.

- **Boat Tours:** Embark on a captivating boat tour and explore the dramatic coastline from a different perspective. Cruise along the Bay of Kotor and marvel at the imposing cliffs, charming villages, and hidden coves. Boat tours often include stops for swimming in secluded bays and snorkeling opportunities, allowing you to experience the beauty of the Adriatic Sea up close.

- **Island Hopping:** Set sail on an island-hopping adventure and discover the hidden gems scattered along the coast. Explore the car-free island of Mamula, a historic fortress offering stunning views and a unique glimpse into Montenegro's past. Visit the serene island of Sveti Nikola, a haven for secluded beaches and crystal-clear waters. Island hopping allows you to experience the diversity of Montenegro's coastline, from historical landmarks to pristine natural beauty.

- **Hiking and Cycling:** For those seeking a more active adventure, the Adriatic Coast offers a network of scenic hiking and cycling trails. Hike along the dramatic cliffs overlooking the turquoise waters, enjoying breathtaking vistas and fresh sea air. Cycle through charming villages, olive groves, and rolling hills, experiencing the beauty of the Montenegrin countryside. Whether you choose a leisurely stroll or a challenging climb, the trails along the Adriatic Coast offer a rewarding way to explore the landscape.

A Culinary Journey

No exploration of Montenegro is complete without indulging in its delicious cuisine. The Adriatic Coast is a haven for fresh seafood, with restaurants serving delectable dishes prepared with locally caught fish, prawns, and squid. Savor succulent grilled octopus, plump mussels steamed in white wine, or a hearty fish stew bursting with flavor. Beyond seafood, Montenegrin cuisine offers savory meats like cevapcici (grilled sausages) and pljeskavica (meat patties), often served with tangy kajmak (clotted cream). Pair your meal with a glass of local Montenegrin wine, produced in the fertile valleys near the coast, for a truly immersive culinary experience.

Festivals and Events

The Adriatic Coast comes alive throughout the year with vibrant festivals and events. Immerse yourself in the Kotor Carnival, a riotous celebration with elaborate costumes, lively parades, and a contagious energy that will leave you exhilarated. In Budva, witness the Sea Dance Festival, a renowned electronic music event that attracts world-class DJs and transforms the town into a buzzing hub of nightlife. For a more traditional experience, attend the Grape Festival in Petrovac, a celebration of the grape harvest with folk music, dancing, and local food specialties. Participating in these festivals allows you to connect with Montenegrin culture and create unforgettable memories.

A Harmonious Blend

The beauty of Montenegro's Adriatic Coast lies in its harmonious blend of natural wonders, rich history, and vibrant culture. Sun-drenched beaches beckon for relaxation, while charming towns whisper tales of a bygone era. The turquoise waters of the Adriatic Sea invite exploration, while dramatic cliffs offer breathtaking vistas. Whether you crave an adrenaline-pumping adventure or a tranquil escape, Montenegro's Adriatic Coast has something for everyone. So, pack your swimsuit, your sense of adventure, and get ready to discover the azure paradise that awaits.

Remember, the captivating beauty of the Adriatic Coast doesn't exist in isolation. It seamlessly blends with the dramatic landscapes of Montenegro's national parks, offering a well-rounded travel experience. After a day of exploring charming coastal towns and basking on pristine beaches, you can venture inland and conquer challenging peaks like Bobotov Kuk in Durmitor National Park, a testament to the country's diverse landscapes. This interplay between the serenity of the coast and the ruggedness of the mountains creates a truly unforgettable travel destination.

Budva vs. Sveti Stefan: A Tale of Two Coasts

Montenegro's Adriatic coastline boasts a captivating duality. Budva, a vibrant resort town, pulsates with energy, while Sveti Stefan, a secluded island, offers an aura of exclusivity and tranquility. Deciding between these two destinations depends on the kind of experience you seek. Let's delve into the distinct vibes of each:

Budva: A Buzzing Hive of Activity

Imagine a town that never sleeps. Budva is a lively hub where energy spills from bustling streets onto pristine beaches. Here's what awaits you:

- **Thriving Atmosphere:** Budva is a party town. Lively bars with open-air terraces teem with people, and music spills out onto the streets. The energy is contagious, perfect for those seeking a vibrant nightlife scene.
- **Modern Amenities:** Budva is a modern resort town catering to all your needs. Choose from a wide range of hotels, from budget-friendly options to luxurious beachfront accommodations. A plethora of restaurants offer international cuisine alongside local delicacies. For

entertainment, you'll find casinos, discos, and a variety of shops selling everything from souvenirs to designer brands.

- **Action-Packed Activities:** Budva isn't just about nightlife. Indulge in water sports like jet skiing, parasailing, or kayaking. Explore the coastline on boat tours or rent a car and discover hidden coves along the scenic route. For a touch of history, delve into the charming Old Town with its narrow cobbled streets and Venetian-influenced architecture.

Sveti Stefan: An Oasis of Exclusivity

Sveti Stefan is the epitome of an exclusive island getaway. Imagine a car-free haven where tranquility reigns supreme:

- **Secluded Tranquility:** Sveti Stefan is a world unto itself. The island itself is a resort, accessible only to guests. This exclusivity fosters a peaceful atmosphere, perfect for those seeking relaxation and privacy.

- **Luxury Accommodations:** Sveti Stefan is synonymous with luxury. The entire island is transformed into a high-end resort, offering impeccable service, luxurious amenities, and breathtaking views of the Adriatic Sea. Imagine lounging by the pool, indulging in spa treatments, and savoring gourmet meals in a setting of unparalleled beauty.

- **Limited Activities:** Sveti Stefan is all about relaxation and soaking up the luxurious ambiance. While you can enjoy swimming, sunbathing, and exploring the island's charming walkways, options for high-octane activities are limited. The focus here is on unwinding and indulging in a sense of serenity.

Choosing Your Escape

The ideal destination depends on your travel style:

- **For the Party Animal:** If you crave a vibrant nightlife scene, a plethora of restaurants and shops, and a constant buzz of activity, Budva is your perfect match. Here, you can find excitement around every corner, from lively bars to action-packed water sports.

- **For the Relaxation Seeker:** If you yearn for a tranquil escape, where luxury reigns supreme and peacefulness is paramount, Sveti Stefan beckons. Indulge in pampering spa treatments, savor gourmet meals, and simply relax amidst breathtaking scenery.

Beyond the Contrast

Despite their distinct vibes, Budva and Sveti Stefan share a common thread – their stunning location on the Adriatic Coast. Both destinations offer access to pristine beaches, turquoise waters, and charming Montenegrin hospitality. Consider combining your trip, experiencing the vibrancy of Budva and the tranquility of Sveti Stefan, creating a well-rounded Montenegrin adventure.

Lakes and Serenity

Montenegro's drape extends beyond dramatic peaks and sun-drenched beaches. Lay close amidst rolling hills and verdant valleys lie captivating lakes, offering a haven for tranquility and a connection with nature. This chapter invites you to experience the serenity of Skadar Lake and Black Lake, two jewels lay close within Montenegro's diverse landscapes.

Skadar Lake: A Birder's Paradise

Imagine gliding across a vast expanse of water, the mirror-like surface reflecting the azure sky and cotton-wool clouds. This is the magic of Skadar Lake, Europe's largest freshwater lake, a haven for diverse birdlife and a place where time seems to slow down. Skadar Lake, shared between Montenegro and Albania, offers a unique ecosystem teeming with over 270 bird species, making it a paradise for birdwatchers and nature enthusiasts alike.

A Peaceful Boat Ride

Embark on a gentle boat ride and discover the hidden beauty of Skadar Lake. As your vessel glides across the water, keep your eyes peeled for a dazzling array of feathered residents. Spot elegant Dalmatian pelicans with their impressive wingspans, graceful white egrets perched on reeds, and shy purple herons camouflaged amongst the lush vegetation. Listen to the symphony of bird calls that fill the air, a reminder of the vibrant life teeming within this ecosystem.

Island Monasteries: Whispers of History

Skadar Lake is not just a haven for birds; it's also dotted with picturesque islands that hold historical significance. Several islands are home to ancient monasteries, silent sentinels standing guard over the lake for centuries. Visit the imposing Monastery of St. Stefan, a 15th-century structure adorned with frescoes and offering a glimpse into Montenegro's rich religious heritage. Explore the serene Monastery of Komsino, lay close amidst olive groves and exuding an aura of peacefulness. As you wander through these monasteries, imagine the lives of monks who dedicated themselves to a life of solitude in this breathtaking setting.

Beyond the Boat

While a boat ride is the quintessential way to experience Skadar Lake, the surrounding area offers other ways to explore:

- **Hiking and Cycling:** Lace up your hiking boots and explore the network of trails that wind through the hills bordering the lake. Enjoy panoramic views of the vast expanse of water and encounter diverse flora and fauna along the way. Alternatively, rent a bicycle and explore the charming villages that dot the lakeshore, immersing yourself in the local way of life.

- **Kayaking and Canoeing:** For a more intimate exploration, rent a kayak or canoe and navigate the hidden coves and inlets of the lake. Paddle through stands of reeds, discover secluded beaches, and experience the tranquility of Skadar Lake from a different perspective.

- **Birdwatching Tours:** Enlist the expertise of a local guide who can help you identify the diverse birdlife inhabiting the lake. Learn about their calls, behaviors, and the vital role they play in this unique ecosystem.

Black Lake: A Cyclist's Delight

Lay close amidst the dramatic peaks of Durmitor National Park lies Black Lake (Crno Jezero), a jewel reflecting the surrounding mountains and offering a picturesque escape. While smaller than Skadar Lake, Black Lake boasts a serene beauty and a plethora of activities for those seeking an active yet peaceful escape.

A Scenic Cycle Ride

Rent a bicycle and embark on a scenic ride around the perimeter of Black Lake. The well-maintained path is perfect for cyclists of all levels, offering breathtaking views of the surrounding mountains and the crystal-clear waters of the lake. As you cycle, breathe in the fresh mountain air, listen to the gentle lapping of waves against the shore, and feel the tranquility of nature envelop you.

Beyond the Cycle Path

Black Lake offers more than just a scenic cycle path:

- **Hiking Adventures:** For the more adventurous, explore the network of hiking trails that lead deeper into Durmitor National Park. These trails offer stunning views of the surrounding peaks, lush forests, and hidden waterfalls, a perfect way to experience the park's diverse landscapes.

- **Swimming and Boating:** During the warm summer months, take a refreshing dip in the cool waters of Black Lake. Alternatively, rent a small boat and explore the lake from a different perspective, enjoying the peacefulness and the breathtaking scenery.

- **Fishing:** Anglers can cast their lines in the lake's pristine waters, hoping to catch trout or carp. Fishing in Black Lake requires a permit, so be sure to obtain one before casting your line.

Exploring Skadar Lake and Black Lake allows you to experience a different side of Montenegro, one steeped in tranquility and natural beauty. These lakes offer a welcome respite from the coastal buzz or the challenging hikes within the national parks. Imagine a day spent exploring the hidden coves of Skadar Lake, spotting elusive birds and marveling at ancient monasteries. The next day, you could be cycling around Black Lake, the crisp mountain air invigorating your senses as you soak in the breathtaking panorama of Durmitor National Park. This ability to seamlessly transition between diverse landscapes is a hallmark of Montenegro's travel experience.

Both Skadar Lake and Black Lake offer unique experiences that resonate with the overall drape of Montenegro. Here's how they connect with what we've explored so far:

- **Connection to Nature:** Just like the national parks, these lakes offer opportunities to immerse yourself in nature. Skadar Lake's diverse birdlife and Black Lake's mountain setting mirror the ecological richness of Montenegro.

- **Historical Significance:** The ancient monasteries on Skadar Lake echo the historical sites found throughout the country, offering a glimpse into Montenegro's rich past.

- **Active Pursuits:** While offering tranquility, both lakes cater to active travelers. Cycling around Black Lake or kayaking through the inlets of Skadar Lake parallels the hiking and water sports available along the Adriatic Coast.

- **Peace and Tranquility:** Exploring these lakes provides a sense of peace and serenity, a perfect counterpoint to the bustling energy of Budva or the adrenaline rush of conquering a mountain peak in Durmitor National Park.

Planning Your Lakeside Escape

Here are some tips for planning your visit to Skadar Lake and Black Lake:

Skadar Lake

- **Best Time to Visit:** Spring (April-May) and fall (September-October) offer pleasant weather and comfortable temperatures for exploring the lake. Birdwatching is particularly rewarding during these seasons.

- **Accommodation:** Several charming villages and towns dot the shores of Skadar Lake, offering a variety of accommodation options, from guesthouses to luxury hotels.

- **Boat Tours:** Numerous boat tours operate on Skadar Lake, offering guided exploration of the islands, monasteries, and birdwatching hotspots.
- **Permits:** Certain areas of Skadar Lake fall within national parks, requiring a park entrance fee. Check with local authorities beforehand.

Black Lake

- **Best Time to Visit:** Summer (June-August) offers warm weather perfect for swimming and enjoying outdoor activities. However, this is also the peak season, so expect larger crowds. Shoulder seasons (May-June and September) offer pleasant weather with fewer crowds.
- **Accommodation:** The charming town of Žabljak serves as the gateway to Durmitor National Park and Black Lake. Here, you'll find a variety of hotels, guesthouses, and apartments to suit your budget.
- **Bicycle Rentals:** Bicycle rentals are readily available near Black Lake, making it easy to explore the scenic path around the perimeter.
- **Hiking Trails:** Pick up a map of Durmitor National Park to explore the various hiking trails leading from Black Lake into the surrounding mountains. Difficulty levels vary, so choose a trail that suits your fitness level.

A Lasting Impression

Skadar Lake and Black Lake offer a captivating escape into the serene heart of Montenegro. Whether you seek to witness a symphony of birdlife, explore ancient monasteries, or cycle around a crystal-clear lake surrounded by mountains, these tranquil havens promise a lasting impression. So, pack your sense of adventure, a thirst for exploration, and get ready to discover the serenity that awaits you amidst Montenegro's captivating lakes.

ECHOES OF EMPIRES: EXPLORING MEDIEVAL TOWNS

Montenegro's drape extends beyond its dramatic landscapes and sun-drenched beaches. The country boasts a rich history, evident in its charming medieval towns, each whispering tales of bygone eras. This chapter invites you on a journey through time, exploring the Venetian-influenced town of Kotor and the Ottoman-kissed Herceg Novi, unveiling the architectural gems and historical significance of these captivating destinations.

Kotor: A Venetian Masterpiece

Step inside the imposing city walls of Kotor, and you'll be transported to a bygone era. Designated a UNESCO World Heritage Site, Kotor's Old Town is a labyrinth of narrow cobbled streets lined with Venetian-influenced architecture, a testament to the town's long and fascinating history.

A Walking Tour Through Time

Imagine yourself embarking on a walking tour, each step revealing a new architectural gem. Start your journey at the grandiose Sea Gate, the main entrance to the Old Town, adorned with the Lion of St. Mark, a symbol of Venetian rule. As you wander through the maze of streets, keep your eyes peeled for the intricate details that define Kotor's architecture. Notice the elegant loggias (open balconies), the ornately carved stone doorways, and the terracotta-roofed houses with their distinctive Venetian windows.

Piazza of Arms: The Heart of the Town

Your exploration leads you to the Piazza of Arms, the heart of Kotor's Old Town. This bustling square is framed by towering Venetian palaces, each one boasting a unique architectural style. Here, you'll find the Clock Tower, its weathered face a silent witness to centuries gone by. Admire the ornate façade of the Prince's

Palace, a symbol of Venetian authority, and marvel at the Cathedral of Saint Tryphon, a Romanesque masterpiece showcasing intricate stonework and sacred treasures.

Climbing the City Walls

For a breathtaking perspective, ascend the imposing city walls that snake their way up the mountainside. The climb might be challenging, but the panoramic views are simply awe-inspiring. Gaze down at the red-tiled roofs of the Old Town spilling down to the turquoise waters of the Bay of Kotor, and imagine the bustling port that Kotor once was, a vital trading post for the Venetian Republic.

Beyond the Walls

While Kotor's Old Town is the star attraction, the town itself offers more to explore:

- **Maritime Museum:** Delve deeper into Kotor's seafaring history by visiting the Maritime Museum, housed within the impressive Grgurin Palace. Here, you'll discover nautical artifacts, ship models, and fascinating exhibits chronicling the town's maritime past.
- **Cats of Kotor:** These furry residents are an integral part of Kotor's charm. Keep an eye out for them basking in the sun or strolling nonchalantly through the streets. A local legend even credits them with saving the town from a plague of rats!

Resonating with the Coast

Kotor's Venetian influence resonates with the overall experience of Montenegro's Adriatic Coast. The charming coastal towns, like Budva, with their terracotta-roofed houses and narrow streets, echo the architectural style found within Kotor's walls. Exploring Kotor allows you to connect the dots, piecing together the historical drape of the region.

Herceg Novi: A Balkan Beauty

Travel south along the coast and discover Herceg Novi, a captivating town lay close amidst lush greenery and overlooking the shimmering Bay of Boka Kotorska. Herceg Novi boasts a distinct charm, a captivating blend of Ottoman and Mediterranean influences.

Unveiling the Hidden Charm

Imagine strolling along the charming pedestrian promenade, lined with cafes and shops, and soaking in the vibrant atmosphere. Admire the imposing Kanli Kula fortress, a formidable Ottoman structure guarding the entrance to the bay. Wander through the labyrinthine streets of the Old Town, a kaleidoscope of architectural styles, where Ottoman mosques stand side-by-side with baroque churches. Take a break in a traditional Turkish hammam and experience a rejuvenating bath, a legacy of Ottoman rule.

A Fortress with a View

No visit to Herceg Novi is complete without exploring the imposing Forte Mare, a majestic fortress perched atop a hill overlooking the bay. Built by the Ottomans in the 14th century, the fortress offers a glimpse into the town's strategic importance. Climb the ramparts and be rewarded with breathtaking panoramic views of the bay, the surrounding mountains, and the charming town lay close below. Forte Mare also houses a fascinating maritime museum, showcasing the region's rich naval history.

Beyond the Town Walls

Herceg Novi offers more than just historical charm:

- **Boat Tours:** Embark on a captivating boat tour and explore the dramatic coastline from a different perspective. Cruise along the Bay of Boka Kotorska, marveling at the imposing cliffs, charming villages, and hidden coves. Boat tours often include stops for swimming in secluded bays and snorkeling opportunities, allowing you to experience the beauty of the Adriatic Sea up close.

- **Botanical Garden:** Immerse yourself in a world of vibrant flora by visiting the Herceg Novi Botanical Garden, one of the oldest in the Mediterranean. Established in the 19th century, the garden boasts a breathtaking collection of plants from around the world, creating a tranquil oasis amidst the town's energy.

- **Škver:** Step back in time and explore Škver, the historic old town harbor. Here, you'll find charming cafes with waterfront terraces, perfect for people-watching and savoring a cup of local coffee. Admire the traditional fishing boats bobbing in the water, and soak in the relaxed atmosphere of this historic port.

Herceg Novi's blend of Ottoman and Mediterranean influences resonates with the overall cultural drape of Montenegro. Just like the coastal towns that reflect Venetian rule, Herceg Novi showcases the lasting impact of the Ottoman Empire on the region's architecture, traditions, and cuisine. Exploring Herceg Novi allows you to experience the rich cultural crossroads that defines Montenegro.

Planning Your Medieval Exploration

Here are some tips for planning your visit to Kotor and Herceg Novi:

Kotor

- **Best Time to Visit:** Spring (April-May) and fall (September-October) offer pleasant weather and comfortable temperatures for exploring the town. The crowds are also smaller during these shoulder seasons.
- **Accommodation:** A variety of hotels, guesthouses, and apartments are available within the Old Town walls or in the newer part of Kotor, offering options for all budgets.
- **City Walls:** Climbing the city walls requires a paid entrance ticket. Wear comfortable shoes and be prepared for a bit of a climb, but the rewards are worth the effort.

Herceg Novi

- **Best Time to Visit:** Spring (April-May) and fall (September-October) offer pleasant weather for exploring the town. The summer months can be hot and crowded.
- **Accommodation:** Herceg Novi offers a wide range of accommodation options, from luxury hotels overlooking the bay to budget-friendly guesthouses within the Old Town.
- **Boat Tours:** Numerous boat tour companies operate in Herceg Novi, offering various itineraries and durations. Choose a tour that suits your interests and budget.

Kotor and Herceg Novi offer a captivating journey through time, unveiling the rich history and cultural drape of Montenegro. From the Venetian grandeur of Kotor to the Ottoman influence in Herceg Novi, these towns promise an unforgettable experience. So, pack your walking shoes, your sense of curiosity, and get ready to discover the echoes of empires that resonate within these captivating medieval towns.

Exploring Kotor and Herceg Novi allows you to connect the dots of your Montenegrin adventure. Imagine a day spent wandering the narrow streets of Kotor, marveling at Venetian architecture, followed by a boat tour along the Bay of Kotor, taking in the dramatic scenery that echoes the coastal towns you've explored. The next day, you could be strolling through the charming squares of Herceg Novi, savoring Turkish coffee and admiring the Ottoman influence, before venturing inland to explore the dramatic peaks of Durmitor National Park, a testament to the country's diverse landscapes. Montenegro offers a journey that seamlessly blends history, nature, and vibrant culture, creating a truly unforgettable travel experience.

Monuments and Museums

Montenegro's charm extends beyond its dramatic coastline and adventure-filled national parks. Lay close amidst the rolling hills of the Lovćen massif lies Cetinje, a captivating town steeped in history and cultural significance. Once the regal capital of Montenegro, Cetinje whispers tales of a bygone era, its museums brimming with national treasures and its streets echoing with the footsteps of kings and queens. Join us on a narrative journey as we unveil the cultural heart of Montenegro in Cetinje, a place where history comes alive.

A Town Steeped in Legacy

Imagine stepping back in time as you enter the charming town of Cetinje. Founded in the 15th century, Cetinje served as the political and cultural center of Montenegro for centuries. The legacy of this bygone era is evident in the town's architecture. Elegant two-story buildings line the main boulevards, their facades adorned with intricate details, while leafy squares provide a sense of tranquility amidst the historical significance. Cetinje is a place where cobbled streets whisper stories of battles fought and diplomatic triumphs achieved.

A Treasure Trove of Museums

Cetinje's true magic lies within its plethora of museums, each one a captivating portal into Montenegro's rich past. Here's a glimpse of some of the cultural gems that await you:

- **National Museum of Montenegro:** Embark on a chronological journey through Montenegrin history at the National Museum. Admire archaeological artifacts dating back to Roman times, delve into the fascinating period of Ottoman rule, and learn about the brave Montenegrin heroes who fought for independence. A collection of stunning 19th-century Montenegrin weaponry and traditional clothing provides a glimpse into the lives of past generations.

- **King Nikola's Palace:** Step inside the opulent King Nikola's Palace, the former residence of the beloved Montenegrin monarch. Marvel at the lavishly decorated rooms, adorned with exquisite furniture, glittering chandeliers, and a mesmerizing collection of European art. The palace offers a fascinating glimpse into the life of royalty and the artistic influences that shaped Montenegro's cultural landscape.

- **Petar II Petrović Njegoš Museum:** Dedicated to Montenegro's most revered historical figure, Prince-Bishop Petar II Petrović-Njegoš, this museum delves into his life and legacy. Njegoš was a poet, philosopher, and political leader who played a pivotal role in shaping Montenegro's national identity. The museum exhibits his personal belongings, manuscripts, and portraits, offering a deeper understanding of this influential figure.

- **Museum of Modern Art:** While steeped in history, Cetinje also embraces contemporary art. The Museum of Modern Art showcases works by renowned Montenegrin artists, offering a glimpse into the country's evolving artistic expression.

Beyond the Museum Walls

Cetinje offers more than just museums to explore:

- **Lovćen National Park:** For a dose of dramatic scenery, venture into the nearby Lovćen National Park. Hike or drive to the imposing mausoleum of Petar II Petrović-Njegoš, perched atop Mount Lovćen, offering breathtaking panoramic views of Montenegro.

- **Cetinje Monastery:** Visit the serene Cetinje Monastery, a spiritual center dating back to the 15th century. Admire the ornate frescoes and religious artifacts, and experience the tranquility that emanates from this sacred space.

- **Local Crafts:** Cetinje is a haven for traditional crafts. Browse through charming shops and discover handcrafted jewelry, embroidered textiles, and hand-painted souvenirs, a perfect way to take a piece of Montenegrin culture home with you.

A Haven for Literature Lovers

Cetinje has long been a haven for literature lovers. The town boasts a prestigious National Library, housing a treasure trove of historical documents and rare books. Several bookstores line the main streets, brimming with works by renowned Montenegrin authors and international classics. Imagine curling up in a charming cafe with a cup of Montenegrin coffee and a captivating book, soaking in the town's literary atmosphere.

Resonating with the Hinterland

Exploring Cetinje allows you to connect the dots of your Montenegrin adventure. Imagine a day spent exploring the bustling coastal towns like Budva, reveling in their vibrant energy and beautiful beaches. The next day, you could be wandering through the serene streets of Cetinje, delving into Montenegro's rich history and cultural heritage. Cetinje acts as a bridge between the country's captivating coastline and the dramatic landscapes of the hinterland, offering a well-rounded travel experience.

A Drape Woven with Time

Cetinje's cultural significance resonates with the overall drape of Montenegro. Just like the ancient monasteries scattered throughout the country and the historical significance imbued within the national parks, Cetinje serves as a custodian of Montenegro's rich past. Exploring its museums allows you to gain a deeper understanding of the struggles, triumphs, and cultural influences that shaped the nation we see today.

A Destination for All Seasons

Cetinje offers a captivating experience year-round:

- **Spring (April-May):** Pleasant weather and blooming flowers create a picturesque atmosphere for exploring the town and surrounding areas.
- **Summer (June-August):** While the crowds might be larger, summer offers the opportunity to enjoy outdoor cafes and cultural events held in the squares.
- **Fall (September-October):** The crowds thin out, and the weather remains comfortable for sightseeing. Fall foliage adds a touch of magic to the surrounding mountains.

- **Winter (November-March):** The town takes on a peaceful charm during the winter months. Wrap up warm and explore the museums at your own pace, savoring the tranquility of the off-season.

Planning Your Royal Rendezvous

Here are some tips for planning your visit to Cetinje:

- **Getting There:** Cetinje is easily accessible by car or bus from other major Montenegrin towns like Budva and Podgorica. If arriving by plane, Tivat Airport is the closest, followed by Podgorica Airport.
- **Accommodation:** Cetinje offers a variety of accommodation options, from charming guesthouses to boutique hotels. Choose one that suits your budget and desired level of comfort.
- **Walking Tour:** A great way to explore Cetinje is to join a walking tour. Local guides can share fascinating insights into the town's history and hidden gems.

A Lasting Impression

Cetinje beckons you to embark on a captivating journey through time. From its museums brimming with national treasures to its streets echoing with the footsteps of royalty, Cetinje offers a unique blend of history, culture, and artistic expression. So, pack your curiosity, a good book to delve into in a charming cafe, and get ready to be enchanted by the cultural heart of Montenegro.

Exploring Cetinje allows you to create a seamless travel experience within Montenegro. Imagine a day spent exploring the museums, delving into the country's rich past. The next day, you could be cycling around the serene Black Lake or hiking through the dramatic peaks of Durmitor National Park, creating a well-rounded adventure that encompasses Montenegro's diverse landscapes, cultural heritage, and outdoor activities. This ability to transition between such contrasting experiences is a hallmark of a truly unforgettable Montenegrin adventure.

Njegoš Mausoleum

Montenegro's drape extends beyond its dramatic coastline and sun-drenched beaches. Lay close amidst the soaring peaks of Lovćen National Park lies a unique landmark – the Njegoš Mausoleum. This imposing structure, dedicated to Montenegro's most revered historical figure, Petar II Petrović-Njegoš (also known as Njegoš), offers a journey that blends breathtaking scenery, historical significance, and a touch of physical challenge. Join us as we embark on a climb to the clouds, reaching the Njegoš Mausoleum and experiencing the awe-inspiring panoramas that await.

The Scenic Ascent

Imagine embarking on a scenic journey towards the Njegoš Mausoleum. Your adventure begins near the charming town of Cetinje, the former royal capital of Montenegro. As you wind your way through the verdant foothills of Lovćen National Park, keep your eyes peeled for captivating vistas. Rolling hills dotted with traditional Montenegrin villages unfold before you, offering a glimpse into the country's rural charm. The air grows cooler as you gain altitude, and the scent of pine fills your senses.

The Switchbacks Begin

The road eventually leads to a series of switchbacks that snake their way up the mountainside. This is where the true adventure begins. For those seeking a physical challenge, consider renting a bicycle and tackling the climb on two wheels. For others, a comfortable car will navigate the winding roads with ease. As you ascend, the switchbacks offer breathtaking glimpses of the valley below, the Adriatic Sea sparkling like a jewel on the horizon on a clear day.

The 461 Steps to Eternity

After a series of exhilarating turns, you'll reach a large parking area marking the final leg of your journey. Here, 461 stone steps stand between you and the Njegoš Mausoleum. Take a deep breath and begin your ascent. Imagine each step taking you closer to a remarkable historical landmark and a breathtaking panorama. As you climb, pause occasionally to catch your breath and admire the ever-expanding vista. The surrounding mountains rise majestically, their peaks often veiled in wispy clouds, creating an air of mystery and grandeur.

Reaching the Eagle's Nest

Finally, after conquering the 461 steps, you'll arrive at the imposing Njegoš Mausoleum. This unique structure, resembling a chapel carved from stone, sits atop Mount Jezerski Vrch, the second-highest peak in Lovćen National Park. Nicknamed "Orlov Krš" (Eagle's Nest) for its lofty perch, the mausoleum embodies Njegoš's spirit – a man who soared above the ordinary, both literally and figuratively.

A Glimpse Inside the Mausoleum

The entrance to the mausoleum is flanked by two imposing statues of Montenegrin women in traditional attire, symbolizing the nation's strength and resilience. Step inside, and a sense of reverence washes over you. The mausoleum's interior is adorned with mosaics and intricate stonework. Njegoš's sarcophagus rests beneath a golden canopy, a fitting tribute to this revered leader.

A Breathtaking Panorama

Step outside the mausoleum and prepare to be awestruck. The panoramic views from this vantage point are simply breathtaking. On a clear day, your gaze sweeps across a vast expanse of territory. The dramatic peaks of Lovćen National Park rise majestically around you, their rugged beauty stealing your breath away. Gaze down at the shimmering expanse of the Adriatic Sea, a dazzling contrast to the emerald green valleys and snow-capped peaks. Imagine the vastness of Montenegro laid out before you, a testament to the country's stunning natural beauty.

Resonating with the Hinterland

Reaching the Njegoš Mausoleum resonates with the overall experience of exploring Montenegro's hinterland. Just like the challenging hikes within Durmitor National Park that reward you with breathtaking vistas, the climb to the mausoleum offers a sense of accomplishment alongside the historical significance and panoramic reward. Exploring the Njegoš Mausoleum allows you to connect the dots of your Montenegrin adventure.

A Drape of History and Nature

The Njegoš Mausoleum is more than just a scenic viewpoint. It's a poignant reminder of Montenegro's rich history and the enduring legacy of Petar II Petrović-Njegoš. Njegoš was a multifaceted figure – a prince-bishop, a poet, and a philosopher who played a pivotal role in shaping Montenegro's national identity. Visiting his mausoleum allows you to pay homage to this influential leader and gain a deeper appreciation for Montenegro's cultural drape.

Planning Your Climb to the Clouds

Here are some tips for planning your climb

- **Choosing Your Season:** The Njegoš Mausoleum is accessible year-round, but the experience varies depending on the season. Spring (April-May) offers pleasant weather and blooming wildflowers, while summer (June-August) can be crowded with tourists. Fall (September-October) provides comfortable temperatures and stunning fall foliage, while winter (November-March) offers a tranquil experience with fewer crowds. However, be aware that the mausoleum might be closed on some days due to heavy snowfall.

- **Gear Up:** Comfortable shoes are essential for navigating the switchbacks and climbing the stairs. If visiting in summer, sunscreen and a hat are crucial. During winter, pack warm layers and waterproof gear as the weather can change rapidly at higher altitudes.

- **Entrance Fees:** There's a small entrance fee for Lovćen National Park and a separate fee to enter the Njegoš Mausoleum. Consider purchasing a combination ticket for better value.

- **Refreshments:** A small café operates near the parking area, offering refreshments and snacks.

While the Njegoš Mausoleum is the main attraction, Lovćen National Park offers additional experiences. Consider exploring the nearby village of Njeguši, Njegoš's birthplace. Here, you can visit his family home and learn more about his early life. Hiking enthusiasts can embark on scenic trails that weave through the park's diverse landscapes. Keep an eye out for the park's rich flora and fauna, including rare birds and wild boars.

Reaching the Njegoš Mausoleum is more than just a scenic drive and a climb. It's a journey that resonates with the spirit of Montenegro. It's about overcoming challenges, appreciating history, and marveling at the country's breathtaking beauty. As you stand atop Mount Jezerski Vrch, basking in the panoramic vista and the rich historical significance, you'll gain a deeper understanding of what makes Montenegro such a captivating destination. So, lace up your shoes, pack your sense of adventure, and embark on your own climb to the clouds. The Njegoš Mausoleum awaits, ready to leave a lasting impression.

Festivals and Traditions

Montenegro's drape extends beyond its dramatic landscapes, sun-drenched beaches, and historical towns. The country bursts with vibrant traditions and a spirit of celebration, particularly evident during its captivating festivals. One such event, the Kotor Carnival, transports you to a world of music, flamboyant costumes, and unbridled joy. Join us as we immerse ourselves in the electrifying atmosphere of the Kotor Carnival, a spectacle that resonates with the cultural heart of Montenegro.

A Celebration Steeped in Tradition

Imagine yourself stepping into the heart of Kotor's Old Town on the cusp of February. A palpable energy fills the air, a buzz of anticipation mingled with the joyous sounds of music. This is the Kotor Carnival, a tradition dating back centuries, when the town transforms into a stage for a captivating spectacle. For three days, locals and visitors alike come together to celebrate, shedding inhibitions and embracing the spirit of revelry.

A Feast for the Eyes: The Costumes

The cornerstone of the Kotor Carnival lies in its dazzling costumes. Wander the cobbled streets and marvel at the creativity on display. Local groups, known as "družine," spend months meticulously crafting elaborate costumes that tell stories, depict historical figures, or simply showcase their flamboyant side. Feathers, sequins, and vibrant colors come together in a kaleidoscope of visual delights. Imagine towering figures adorned with mythical creatures' masks, mischievous jesters prancing through the crowds, and elegant ladies in bygone-era attire, each adding to the captivating atmosphere.

The Pulse of the Carnival: Music and Dance

Music serves as the lifeblood of the Kotor Carnival. Energetic brass bands fill the air with lively tunes, while traditional instruments like gusle (a one-stringed fiddle) and flutes lend a touch of local flavor. The rhythmic beats draw you in, and it's near impossible to resist the urge to tap your feet or sway to the music. As the energy builds, impromptu dance parties erupt in the squares, a joyful expression of community spirit.

A Journey Through Time: The Catana Procession

One of the highlights of the Kotor Carnival is the Catana Procession. This unique event pays homage to the town's rich history and its Venetian heritage. Participants, dressed in traditional Venetian costumes, parade through the streets, their faces obscured by elaborate masks. Imagine the rhythmic clang of swords and the echoing footsteps as the procession winds its way through the town, a captivating glimpse into Kotor's Venetian past.

A Carnival for All

The Kotor Carnival caters to all ages and interests. Children delight in chasing costumed characters and participating in fun games organized in the squares. Adults revel in the infectious energy, soaking in the music, and indulging in delicious local treats sold by street vendors. The atmosphere is inclusive and welcoming, creating a sense of camaraderie amongst locals and visitors alike.

Resonating with the Cultural Drape

The Kotor Carnival resonates with the overall cultural drape of Montenegro. Just like the traditional celebrations held in villages throughout the country, the carnival showcases the importance of community, music, and storytelling in Montenegrin culture. Participating in the Kotor Carnival allows you to experience this vibrant spirit firsthand, creating memories that will last a lifetime.

Beyond the Festivities

While the Kotor Carnival is the main event, your exploration of Montenegrin culture can extend far beyond these three days. Here are some ways to delve deeper:

- **Visit Local Museums:** Museums across Montenegro, like the National Museum of Montenegro in Cetinje, offer fascinating insights into the country's history, traditions, and artistic heritage.

- **Experience Local Crafts:** Explore charming shops throughout Montenegro and discover traditional crafts like embroidery, pottery, and jewelry making. Consider purchasing a unique souvenir handcrafted by local artisans.

- **Learn a Few Montenegrin Phrases:** A few basic phrases in Montenegrin will go a long way in showing respect for the local culture and enhancing your interactions with friendly locals.

- **Attend Local Festivals:** Montenegro hosts a variety of festivals throughout the year, celebrating everything from wine and music to traditional dance and folklore. Research upcoming events and immerse yourself in the local spirit.

A Celebration of Life

The Kotor Carnival is more than just a vibrant display of costumes and music. It's a celebration of life, a time to shed inhibitions, embrace community spirit, and revel in the joy of shared experiences. As you participate in the festivities, you'll gain a deeper appreciation for the warmth and hospitality that define Montenegrin culture.

Connecting the Dots of Your Adventure

Imagine a day spent exploring the captivating medieval town of Kotor, marveling at its Venetian architecture and rich history. In the afternoon, the energy shifts as the Kotor Carnival explodes into life. Vibrant costumes fill the streets, music fills the air, and the infectious joy of the celebration draws you in. Participating in the Kotor Carnival allows you to connect the dots of your Montenegrin adventure. Just like exploring the serene monasteries lay close amidst dramatic landscapes, the carnival pulsates with the essence of Montenegro – a country that celebrates its heritage while embracing the present.

A Seamless Journey

The beauty of Montenegro lies in its ability to offer a diverse range of experiences within a relatively compact region. Imagine contrasting your experience at the Kotor Carnival with a peaceful hike through the verdant trails of Lovćen National Park, or a day spent soaking up the sun on a pristine beach along the Budva Riviera. This seamless transition between cultural immersion, historical exploration, and outdoor adventure is what makes Montenegro a truly unforgettable destination.

A Lasting Impression

The Kotor Carnival leaves a lasting impression long after the music fades and the costumes are put away. It's a reminder of the importance of celebrating life, of embracing traditions, and of connecting with people from all walks of life. As you depart from Kotor, the echoes of laughter and the vibrant colors of the carnival will linger in your memory, a testament to the captivating spirit of Montenegro.

Planning Your Carnival Adventure

The Kotor Carnival typically takes place over three days in late February. Here are some tips for planning your visit:

- **Accommodation:** Book your accommodation well in advance, especially if traveling during peak season. Kotor's Old Town offers a variety of charming hotels and guesthouses, but these fill up quickly during the carnival.
- **Weather:** February in Montenegro can be unpredictable. Pack layers of clothing and be prepared for rain.
- **Embrace the Spirit:** Come ready to participate! Wear a colorful costume (optional but adds to the fun), learn a few basic dance moves, and most importantly, embrace the joyful spirit of the carnival.

The Kotor Carnival beckons you to experience the vibrant heart of Montenegro. Immerse yourself in the electrifying atmosphere, marvel at the dazzling costumes, and let the music move you. This captivating festival is just one thread in the rich drape that is Montenegro. So, pack your bags, a sense of adventure, and get ready to be swept away by the magic of the Kotor Carnival.

Grape Festival

Montenegro's charm extends beyond its dramatic landscapes and sun-drenched beaches. Lay close amidst rolling hills and fertile valleys lies a tradition deeply rooted in the country's identity – winemaking. This rich heritage is celebrated with vibrant gusto at the Grape Festival, a captivating event that blends local delicacies, traditional grape stomping, and a festive atmosphere. Join us as we delve into the significance of the Grape Festival, an experience that resonates with the essence of Montenegro.

A Toast to Tradition

Imagine yourself strolling through the charming village of Virpazar on the shores of Lake Skadar. The air is buzzing with excitement, a prelude to the much-anticipated Grape Festival. This annual celebration, held in September, marks the culmination of the grape harvest, a time to give thanks for a bountiful season and celebrate the fruits (literally) of the land. For generations, the Grape Festival has been a cornerstone of Montenegrin tradition, a vibrant expression of the country's deep connection to winemaking.

A Journey Through Time: The Grape Stomping Ceremony

The highlight of the Grape Festival is the captivating grape stomping ceremony. This age-old tradition, practiced for centuries, is a messy yet exhilarating experience. Participants, clad in traditional clothing, wade into large wooden vats overflowing with ripe grapes. With laughter and joyous shouts, they stomp on the grapes, releasing the sweet nectar that will be transformed into delicious wine. Imagine the energy swirling around you as the air fills with the intoxicating scent of freshly crushed grapes, a visual and sensory representation of the winemaking process. The grape stomping ceremony is more than just a fun activity; it's a symbolic act that connects the present generation to the legacy of their ancestors.

A Feast for the Senses: Local Delicacies

The Grape Festival isn't just about wine; it's a celebration of all things delicious. Local vendors line the streets, offering a mouthwatering array of traditional Montenegrin fare. Sink your teeth into flaky pastries filled with savory cheese or sweet jams. Sample regional specialties like "pršuta" (air-dried ham) and "sir" (cheese) made from local sheep's milk. Don't miss the chance to try "lješnica," a sweet cornbread often served warm and drizzled with honey, a perfect way to balance the savory flavors. As you savor these culinary delights, soak in the festive atmosphere, and witness the pride local producers take in showcasing their heritage.

A Toast to Local Wines

Of course, no Grape Festival is complete without sampling the region's renowned wines. Local wineries set up stalls, offering visitors the opportunity to taste a variety of varietals. From crisp white wines perfect for a warm summer day to bold reds ideal for a cozy evening, there's something for every palate. As you swirl the wine in your glass and savor its complex flavors, imagine the dedication and skill of the local winemakers who transform the humble grape into these delicious beverages.

Resonating with the Hinterland

The Grape Festival resonates with the overall experience of exploring Montenegro's hinterland. Just like visiting charming villages lay close amidst rolling hills and traditional farms dotting the countryside, the festival offers a glimpse into a way of life deeply connected to the land. Exploring the Grape Festival allows you to connect the dots of your Montenegrin adventure.

A Drape Woven with Tradition

The Grape Festival is more than just a celebration of wine. It's a vibrant drape woven with tradition, community spirit, and a sense of pride in local agriculture. Participating in the festival allows you to experience this rich heritage firsthand and gain a deeper appreciation for the role winemaking plays in Montenegrin culture.

Beyond the Festival

While the Grape Festival is a highlight, your exploration of Montenegrin winemaking can extend far beyond these festive days. Here are some ways to delve deeper:

- **Visit a Local Winery:** Many wineries in Montenegro offer tours and tastings, allowing you to learn about the winemaking process from grape to bottle.
- **Explore Wine Routes:** Montenegro boasts several designated wine routes, taking you on a scenic journey through vineyards and charming villages.
- **Dine at a Traditional Restaurant:** Pair your meal with a local wine at a traditional restaurant. Many restaurants showcase regional specialties and offer knowledgeable staff who can help you choose the perfect wine pairing.

A Celebration of Community

The Grape Festival is a celebration of community. It's a time for families and friends to come together, share stories, and enjoy the fruits of their labor. As you witness the joyful interactions and the infectious laughter that fills the air, you'll gain a deeper understanding of the importance of community spirit in Montenegro.

A Seamless Journey

The beauty of Montenegro lies in its ability to offer a diverse range of experiences within a compact region. Imagine contrasting your experience at the Grape Festival with a day spent exploring the dramatic peaks of Durmitor National Park, or a relaxing afternoon soaking up the sun on a pristine beach along the Budva Riviera. This seamless transition between indulging in local traditions, exploring the captivating landscapes, and enjoying the coastal charm is what makes Montenegro a truly unforgettable destination.

A Toast to Lasting Memories

The Grape Festival leaves a lasting impression long after the last grape has been stomped and the final sip of wine has been savored. It's a reminder of the importance of celebrating tradition, the joy of shared experiences, and the delicious rewards of a bountiful harvest. As you depart from the festival, the vibrant colors, the infectious laughter, and the lingering taste of local wine will stay with you, a testament to the captivating spirit of Montenegro.

Planning Your Grape Adventure

The Grape Festival typically takes place in mid-September in the charming village of Virpazar. Here are some tips for planning your visit:

- **Accommodation:** Book your accommodation well in advance, especially if traveling during peak season. Virpazar and surrounding towns offer a variety of accommodation options, from charming guesthouses to waterfront hotels.
- **Weather:** September in Montenegro offers pleasant weather, perfect for enjoying the outdoor festivities.
- **Embrace the Spirit:** Come prepared to participate! Wear comfortable clothing and shoes suitable for navigating the festival grounds. Don't be shy to join in the grape stomping (optional but adds to the fun), sample the local delicacies, and soak in the festive atmosphere.

The Grape Festival beckons you to raise a glass to the essence of Montenegro. Immerse yourself in the vibrant celebration, witness the age-old tradition of grape stomping, and savor the delicious local fare. This captivating festival is just one sip in the rich drape of Montenegrin experiences. So, pack your bags, a sense of adventure, and get ready to be swept away by the charm and warmth of the Grape Festival.

Part 2: Embark on an Adventure
HITTING THE TRAILS: HIKING, BIKING, AND OUTDOOR ACTIVITIES IN MONTENEGRO

Hiking Adventures in Durmitor National Park

Montenegro's drape extends far beyond its shimmering coastline and charming towns. Jagged peaks pierce the azure sky, beckoning adventurous souls to explore the dramatic landscapes of Durmitor National Park. Nicknamed the "Roof of Montenegro," Durmitor offers a paradise for hikers of all levels, with trails that weave through alpine meadows, glacial lakes, and soaring mountains. Join me, an avid hiker, as I share my personal experience conquering a challenging hike in Durmitor, along with valuable tips and a detailed breakdown of guided tours available in the park. Get ready to lace up your boots and embark on a journey that resonates with the adventurous spirit of Montenegro.

A Personal Ascent: Bobotov Kuk

The crisp morning air invigorated my senses as I stood at the base of Bobotov Kuk, the highest peak in Durmitor National Park. Towering at 2,525 meters (8,284 ft), Bobotov Kuk is a magnet for ambitious hikers, myself included. The initial ascent was manageable, a gentle incline through a verdant forest. But soon, the path transformed into a series of rocky switchbacks, testing my endurance. Doubt began to creep in as I battled fatigue and questioned my ability to reach the summit. Yet, the breathtaking panoramas that unfolded with each step fueled my determination. Emerald valleys dotted with glacial lakes stretched out below, a reminder of the beauty that awaited at the top.

Overcoming Obstacles, One Step at a Time

As the path became steeper and more challenging, I adopted a simple mantra: "One step at a time." Focusing on the immediate task at hand helped me conquer the mental hurdle and persevere. Taking short breaks to savor the invigorating mountain air and the awe-inspiring scenery also proved invaluable. When exhaustion threatened to overwhelm me, I found encouragement in the camaraderie of fellow hikers, a silent understanding passing between us as we shared this challenging journey.

The Elation of Reaching the Summit

Finally, after hours of climbing, I crested the final ridge and stood atop Bobotov Kuk. The world seemed to stretch out endlessly before me. A wave of exhilaration washed over me, erasing every ounce of fatigue. The breathtaking panorama that unfolded was a reward beyond measure. Jagged peaks pierced the sky, while glacial lakes shimmered like sapphires lay close amidst the emerald valleys. In that moment, I understood why Bobotov Kuk is aptly named the "Roof of Montenegro."

Resonating with the Hinterland

Conquering Bobotov Kuk resonated with the overall experience of exploring Montenegro's hinterland. Just like the scenic drives through Lovćen National Park leading to the Njegoš Mausoleum, the challenging hike to Bobotov Kuk offered a sense of accomplishment alongside breathtaking scenery and a connection with nature. Hiking in Durmitor National Park allows you to connect the dots of your Montenegrin adventure, showcasing the diverse range of experiences this captivating country offers.

Beyond the Personal Challenge: Guided Hiking Tours in Durmitor National Park

While Bobotov Kuk offers an exhilarating challenge for experienced hikers, Durmitor National Park caters to all levels of experience with a variety of guided hiking tours. Here's a breakdown of some popular options:

For the Leisurely Explorer

- **Black Lake Loop:** This easy 4-kilometer (2.5-mile) trail around Black Lake (Crno Jezero) is a perfect introduction to Durmitor's beauty. The flat, well-maintained path offers stunning views of the glacial lake and the surrounding mountains. This tour is ideal for families and those seeking a gentle introduction to the park's scenery.

- **Tara Canyon Rim Hike:** This moderate 8-kilometer (5-mile) trail follows the rim of the dramatic Tara Canyon, the second deepest canyon in Europe. The path offers breathtaking vistas of the canyon walls plunging down towards the emerald Tara River. This tour is a great option for those seeking moderate exercise and stunning scenery.

For the Adventurous Soul

- **Crveno Jezero (Red Lake) Hike:** This moderate-to-challenging 8-kilometer (5-mile) trail leads to the secluded Red Lake (Crveno Jezero), known for its vibrant red color. The path traverses through meadows and forests, eventually reaching a dramatic glacial cirque where the lake lies lay close. This tour is ideal for those seeking a more challenging hike with a unique payoff.

- **Škrčka Lakes Hike:** This challenging 15-kilometer (9.3-mile) trail leads to the Škrčka Lakes glacial basin, a cluster of pristine lakes surrounded by towering peaks. The path involves steep climbs and descents, testing yourendurance. This tour is recommended for experienced hikers seeking a truly rewarding challenge.

For the Peak Baggers

- **Bobotov Kuk Summit:** This challenging 8-kilometer (5-mile) roundtrip hike is the ultimate test for experienced hikers. The path involves steep climbs, exposed sections with fixed cables, and requires a good head for heights. This tour is only recommended for those with excellent physical fitness and a strong sense of adventure. **Benefits of Guided Tours:** Joining a guided hiking tour in Durmitor National Park offers several benefits:

- **Expert Guidance:** Experienced guides ensure your safety on the trails, navigate challenging sections, and share their knowledge about the park's flora, fauna, and history.

- **Safety First:** Guides carry first-aid kits and are trained to handle emergencies, providing peace of mind for even novice hikers.

- **Hidden Gems:** Guides often know secret viewpoints and off-the-beaten-path locations, enriching your experience with hidden gems.

- **Group Camaraderie:** Hiking with a group can be a fun and social experience, allowing you to connect with fellow nature enthusiasts.

Choosing the Right Tour

Here are some things to consider when choosing a guided hiking tour in Durmitor National Park:

- **Your Fitness Level:** Be honest about your physical capabilities and choose a tour that matches your experience level.
- **Duration and Difficulty:** Consider the length and difficulty of the hike, ensuring it aligns with your available time and fitness level.
- **Interests:** Some tours focus on specific aspects like lake exploration, peak ascents, or wildflower viewing. Choose a tour that caters to your interests.
- **Group Size:** Smaller groups offer a more personalized experience, while larger groups can be more social. Choose the setting that suits you best.

Planning Your Hiking Adventure

Here are some additional tips for planning your hiking adventure in Durmitor National Park:

- **Gear Up:** Come prepared with proper hiking boots, weather-appropriate clothing, a backpack, sunscreen, insect repellent, and plenty of water.
- **Check the Weather:** Montenegro's weather can be unpredictable, so check the forecast before your hike.
- **Respect the Park:** Leave no trace, minimize your impact on the environment, and respect the park's regulations. **A Journey of Discovery:**

Hiking in Durmitor National Park is more than just a physical challenge; it's a journey of discovery. It's about pushing your limits, experiencing the raw beauty of nature, and connecting with the wild heart of Montenegro. Whether you choose a leisurely stroll around Black Lake or a challenging ascent of Bobotov Kuk, Durmitor National Park offers an unforgettable experience for every hiker. So, lace up your boots, embrace the spirit of adventure, and get ready to conquer your own "Roof of Montenegro."

Imagine combining your exhilarating hike in Durmitor National Park with a visit to the charming village of Žabljak, the gateway to the park. Here, you can savor delicious Montenegrin cuisine, soak in the local atmosphere, and learn more about the park's rich history. Perhaps you'll even catch a glimpse of wild bears or chamois roaming the park's vast expanse, further enriching your connection with Montenegro's natural wonders.

Hiking in Durmitor National Park will leave a lasting impression long after your return home. The sense of accomplishment, the breathtaking scenery, and the connection with nature will stay with you, a reminder of the captivating spirit of Montenegro. So, pack your bags, a sense of adventure, and get ready to be swept away by the beauty and challenges of Durmitor National Park.

Cycling Paradise: Exploring the Coast and Mountains on Two Wheels

Montenegro transcends the image of a sun-drenched haven. Beyond the shimmering coastline and charming towns lies a paradise for cyclists, offering routes that cater to all levels of experience. Imagine cruising along the picturesque Adriatic coast, the salty breeze in your hair and the turquoise water sparkling beside you. Or, picture yourself conquering challenging mountain trails in Durmitor National Park, surrounded by dramatic landscapes. Whether you're a seasoned cyclist or a weekend enthusiast, Montenegro promises an unforgettable cycling adventure. Join us as we delve into the diverse cycling experiences this captivating country offers, resonating with the spirit of exploration that defines Montenegro.

A Coastal Cruise: Unveiling Hidden Gems

The sun warms your back as you cycle along the scenic coastal route, the sound of waves crashing against the shore your constant companion. This leisurely ride, perfect for cyclists of all abilities, unfolds like a postcard come to life. Charming villages like Budva and Sveti Stefan, with their terracotta rooftops and ancient fortifications, beckon you to explore their narrow cobbled streets. Pause for a refreshing drink at a waterfront café, soaking in the laid-back atmosphere and the mesmerizing views of the Adriatic Sea.

Beyond the Main Road

The beauty of this coastal route lies in its hidden gems. Venture off the main road and discover secluded coves with pristine beaches, perfect for a refreshing dip in the crystal-clear waters. Follow charming backroads that weave through olive groves and vineyards, offering glimpses into the local way of life. Keep an eye out for historical landmarks like crumbling medieval towers and abandoned monasteries, remnants of a rich past whispering stories in the salty breeze.

Resonating with the Hinterland

Cycling along the coast resonates with the overall experience of exploring Montenegro's diverse regions. Just like embarking on a road trip that winds its way through charming villages and dramatic landscapes, this coastal cycling route allows you to connect the dots of your Montenegrin adventure. Imagine contrasting your leisurely coastal ride with a day spent exploring the Bay of Kotor's hidden coves by boat, or indulging in a seafood feast at a charming waterfront restaurant.

Conquering the Mountains: A Challenge for the Avid Cyclist

For the adrenaline seekers and mountain biking enthusiasts, Montenegro offers a different kind of cycling paradise. Durmitor

National Park, with its dramatic peaks and rugged terrain, beckons with challenging single-track trails that test your skills and endurance. Imagine navigating switchbacks that climb through dense forests, your heart pounding with exertion as you ascend towards breathtaking vistas. The sense of accomplishment at reaching the summit, rewarded by panoramic views of the surrounding mountains and valleys, is unparalleled.

Taming Lovćen's Slopes

Lovćen National Park also offers a thrilling challenge for mountain bikers. The trails here wind their way through historical landmarks like the Njegoš Mausoleum, providing a unique blend of physical exertion and cultural immersion. Be prepared for steep climbs and technical descents that demand focus and skill. But the reward? Unforgettable views of the dramatic Montenegrin landscape and a sense of exhilaration that lingers long after the ride is over.

Tips for Mountain Bikers

- **Choose the right gear:** A sturdy mountain bike, a well-fitting helmet, and proper hydration are essential.

- **Plan your route:** Research trails that match your skill level and physical fitness.

- **Be prepared for the elements:** Montenegro's weather can be unpredictable, so pack layers and check the forecast before your ride.

- **Respect the environment:** Stick to designated trails and minimize your impact on the park's natural beauty.

- **Consider a guide:** A knowledgeable guide can enhance your experience, navigate challenging sections, and offer insights into the park's history and flora.

A Seamless Journey

The beauty of cycling in Montenegro lies in its seamless transition between contrasting landscapes. Imagine contrasting your challenging mountain bike adventure in Durmitor National Park with a relaxing afternoon spent soaking up the sun on a pristine beach along the Budva Riviera. This variety of experiences is what makes Montenegro a truly unforgettable cycling destination.

Cycling in Montenegro is more than just a physical activity; it's a journey of discovery. It's about exploring hidden coves along the scenic coastline, conquering challenging mountain trails, and experiencing the breathtaking beauty of the country at your own pace. Whether you choose a leisurely coastal cruise or a heart-pounding mountain ascent, Montenegro offers a cycling adventure that resonates with your sense of adventure. So, grab your helmet, pump up your tires, and get ready to explore Montenegro on two wheels.

Connecting the Dot

Imagine combining your exhilarating cycling adventure with a visit to a local winery in the hinterland. Sample delicious Montenegrin wines produced from grapes grown in the very valleys you cycled through. Learn about the traditional winemaking process and savor the flavors, a perfect way to unwind after a challenging ride. Perhaps you'll even enjoy a traditional Montenegrin meal at a family-run restaurant, the warm hospitality and delicious food adding another layer to your cultural immersion.

A Lasting Impression

Cycling through Montenegro will leave a lasting impression long after your return home. The vivid memories of pedaling along the scenic coastline, the challenging yet exhilarating mountain trails, and the breathtaking scenery will stay with you, a reminder of the captivating spirit of this Balkan nation. So, pack your bags, a sense of adventure, and get ready to be swept away by the diverse cycling experiences that Montenegro offers.

Planning Your Cycling Adventure

Here are some additional tips for planning your cycling adventure in Montenegro:

- **Choosing the Right Time:** Spring (April-May) and fall (September-October) offer pleasant temperatures for cycling, while summer (June-August) can be hot, especially inland.

- **Renting a Bike:** Numerous shops rent bikes in popular tourist destinations. Choose a bike that suits your needs and ensure it's in good working order.

- **Cycling Rules:** Cyclists are required to wear helmets in urban areas. Be aware of traffic regulations and ride defensively.

- **Respecting Local Customs:** Be courteous to pedestrians and fellow cyclists. Yield the right of way when necessary.

Montenegro beckons you to explore its diverse landscapes on two wheels. Whether you're a seasoned cyclist seeking challenging climbs or a leisurely rider enjoying the coastal scenery, this captivating country offers an unforgettable cycling adventure. So, pack your bags, a sense of adventure, and get ready to experience Montenegro's magic, pedal stroke by pedal stroke.

White-Water Rafting on the Tara River, Kayaking on Skadar Lake

Montenegro's drape extends beyond charming villages and dramatic mountains. This captivating country boasts a network of waterways that offer exhilarating adventures for water enthusiasts. Imagine navigating the churning rapids of the Tara River, adrenaline coursing through your veins as you conquer white water. Or, picture yourself gliding across the serene waters of Skadar Lake, surrounded by a symphony of birdsong and the chance to encounter elusive wildlife. Join us as we delve into the aquatic adventures that await in Montenegro, experiences that resonate with the spirit of exploration that defines this Balkan nation.

Conquering the Tara River: A Heart-Pounding Adventure

The morning mist hangs low over the Tara Canyon as you gear up for your white-water rafting adventure. The air crackles with anticipation as your guide briefs you on the route and safety protocols. Then, with a push from the riverbank, your raft plunges into the icy water. The world transforms into a blur of churning whitewater and adrenaline.

Navigating the Rapids

The Tara River, nicknamed "The Tear of Europe," is a playground for white-water enthusiasts. One moment you're paddling calmly through serene stretches of emerald water, the next you're battling through exhilarating rapids with names like "Vrelo" (Boiling Pot) and "Šumovito" (Foamy). Each rapid presents a unique challenge, demanding teamwork and precise maneuvering to navigate the churning water.

A Symphony of Nature

As your heart pounds with exhilaration, take a moment to appreciate the breathtaking scenery that unfolds around you. Towering limestone cliffs, sculpted by millennia of erosion, rise majestically from the riverbank. Dense forests, teeming with life, cling to the canyon walls, providing a cool canopy overhead. The roar of the rapids blends with the calls of unseen birds, creating a symphony of nature that adds to the thrilling experience.

Resonating with the Hinterland

Conquering the Tara River resonates with the overall experience of exploring Montenegro's hinterland. Just like driving through the winding roads of Durmitor National Park, white-water rafting offers a thrilling immersion into the heart of nature. Imagine contrasting your exhilarating rafting adventure with a visit to a traditional village lay close amidst rolling hills, where the locals offer warm hospitality and a glimpse into a slower pace of life.

A Serene Escape: Kayaking on Skadar Lake

After the adrenaline rush of white-water rafting, Skadar Lake offers a serene counterpoint. Imagine gliding across the crystal-clear waters of this vast freshwater lake, the largest in the Balkans. The gentle lapping of waves against your kayak is the only sound that breaks the peaceful silence.

A Paradise for Birdwatchers

Skadar Lake is a haven for birdwatchers. Over 270 species call this lake home, creating a symphony of bird calls that fills the air. Keep an eye out for majestic pelicans gliding gracefully on the water, or spot the elusive purple heron perched on a lily pad. The vibrant kingfisher, with its electric blue plumage, might flit past, adding a splash of color to the scene.

Encountering Elusive Wildlife

As you paddle through the reeds and hidden coves, you might be lucky enough to encounter otters frolicking in the water. These playful creatures are native to the lake, and a glimpse of their sleek bodies is a cherished experience for nature lovers.

A Moment of Reflection

Skadar Lake offers a moment of reflection amidst the adventure-filled journey through Montenegro. As you paddle across the glassy surface, surrounded by breathtaking scenery, you can connect with the tranquility of nature and appreciate the beauty of this captivating country.

Kayaking on Skadar Lake resonates with the overall experience of exploring Montenegro's hinterland. Just like visiting the charming village of Virpazar on the shores of the lake and indulging in a delicious fish feast, kayaking offers a peaceful immersion into the natural beauty of the region. Imagine contrasting your serene kayaking experience with a hike through the nearby wetlands, where you can observe a diverse array of flora and fauna.

A Seamless Journey

The beauty of exploring Montenegro by water lies in the seamless transition between contrasting experiences. Imagine contrasting your exhilarating white-water rafting adventure on the Tara River with a relaxing day spent kayaking on the serene waters of Skadar Lake. This variety of aquatic adventures is what makes Montenegro a truly unforgettable destination for water enthusiasts.

A Journey of Discovery on the Water

Exploring Montenegro by water is more than just a thrilling activity; it's a journey of discovery. It's about navigating the heart-pounding rapids of the Tara River, experiencing the serenity of Skadar Lake, and encountering the diverse wildlife that calls these waterways home. Whether you're a seasoned kayaker seeking a peaceful paddle or an adrenaline junky ready to conquer white water, Montenegro offers an aquatic adventure that resonates with your sense of adventure. So, pack your swimsuit, a sense of exploration, and get ready to experience the magic of Montenegro from a unique perspective.

Imagine combining your thrilling white-water rafting adventure with a visit to the charming town of Žabljak, the gateway to Durmitor National Park. Here, you can savor a hearty Montenegrin meal featuring locally-sourced ingredients, the perfect way to refuel after conquering the Tara River. Perhaps you'll even browse the local markets and find unique handcrafted souvenirs, a tangible reminder of your exhilarating experience.

Exploring Montenegro by water will leave a lasting impression long after your return home. The vivid memories of navigating the Tara River's rapids, the tranquility of kayaking on Skadar Lake, and the encounters with elusive wildlife will stay with you, a reminder of the captivating spirit of this Balkan nation. So, pack your bags, a sense of adventure, and get ready to be swept away by the diverse aquatic experiences that Montenegro offers.

Planning Your Aquatic Adventure

Here are some additional tips for planning your aquatic adventure in Montenegro:

- **Choosing the Right Time:** For white-water rafting, spring (April-May) offers the highest water levels and most thrilling rapids. For kayaking, summer (June-August) provides pleasant weather for exploring Skadar Lake.
- **Rafting Companies:** Numerous reputable companies offer guided white-water rafting trips on the Tara River. Choose one with experienced guides and a good safety record.
- **Kayaking Rentals:** Kayaks can be rented at various locations around Skadar Lake. Consider hiring a guide for a

more personalized experience and to learn about the lake's ecology.

- **Safety First:** Always wear a life jacket when exploring waterways. Be aware of weather conditions and water levels before embarking on your adventure.

A World of Water Awaits

Montenegro's waterways beckon you to explore their diverse offerings. Whether you crave the adrenaline rush of white-water rafting or the serene beauty of kayaking, this captivating country offers an unforgettable aquatic adventure. So, pack your bags, a sense of adventure, and get ready to discover Montenegro from a whole new perspective, one paddle stroke or rapid at a time!

Part 3: A Culinary Journey
FRESH FLAVORS FROM LAND AND SEA

Seafood Delights

Your Montenegrin adventure wouldn't be complete without succumbing to the allure of its fresh seafood. Imagine the salty breeze wafting through your hair as you dine at a charming seaside konoba, a traditional tavern specializing in local delicacies. The vibrant atmosphere, filled with laughter and the clinking of glasses, sets the stage for an unforgettable culinary experience. Join us as we delve into the world of Montenegrin seafood, a symphony of flavors that resonates with the country's rich culinary heritage and coastal charm.

A Feast for the Senses at a Seaside Konoba

The sun dips below the horizon, painting the sky in fiery hues as you arrive at a quaint seaside konoba. The warm glow spilling from the windows beckons you inside. The aroma of grilled seafood mingles with the scent of fresh herbs, instantly whetting your appetite. Friendly staff greets you with a welcoming smile, eager to share the bounty of the Adriatic.

A Celebration of Fresh Catches

The menu boasts a dazzling array of fresh catches, each reflecting the daily offerings of the sea. Succulent plump mussels steamed in white wine and garlic, their briny essence mingling with the fragrant herbs, might be your starter. Perhaps you'll opt for tender calamari, lightly floured and fried to a golden crisp, or indulge in plump Adriatic prawns simply grilled and drizzled with olive oil and lemon juice.

Local Specialties Take Center Stage

As the main course arrives, the true stars of Montenegrin seafood cuisine take center stage. **Black risotto**, a local specialty, might be your choice. This dish is a symphony of textures and flavors, featuring squid ink that lends a dramatic black hue and a subtle, almost sweet, taste to the creamy rice. Fresh seafood like mussels, clams, and shrimp add a burst of briny goodness, while local herbs and spices round out the experience.

Resonating with the Hinterland

Indulging in fresh seafood at a seaside konoba resonates with the overall experience of exploring Montenegro. Just like venturing through charming villages lay close amidst rolling hills and vineyards, a meal at a konoba offers a glimpse into the local way of life. Imagine contrasting your delicious seafood feast with a visit to a traditional farm, where you can witness the production of cheese, olives, and other ingredients that find their way onto Montenegrin tables.

A Taste of Montenegro: Mussels Buzara

For those yearning to recreate a taste of Montenegro at home, here's a recipe for **Mussels Buzara**, a popular and flavorful dish:

Ingredients

- 2 lbs (1 kg) fresh mussels, scrubbed and debearded
- 1/2 cup (120 ml) dry white wine
- 1/4 cup (60 ml) olive oil
- 1 onion, finely chopped
- 2 cloves garlic, minced

- 1 red bell pepper, diced
- 1 Roma tomato, diced
- 1 tbsp (15 ml) tomato paste
- 1/2 tsp (2.5 ml) dried oregano
- 1/4 tsp (1.25 ml) red pepper flakes (optional)
- 1/4 cup (60 ml) chopped fresh parsley
- Salt and freshly ground black pepper to taste

Instructions

1. In a large pot, heat olive oil over medium heat. Add the onion and cook until softened, about 5 minutes.
2. Stir in the garlic, bell pepper, and tomato. Cook for an additional 2-3 minutes, until the vegetables begin to soften.
3. Add the white wine, tomato paste, oregano, and red pepper flakes (if using). Bring to a simmer and cook for 5 minutes.
4. Add the mussels to the pot and stir to coat them in the sauce. Cover the pot tightly and cook for 5-7 minutes, or until the mussels open. Discard any mussels that remain closed.
5. Season with salt and freshly ground black pepper to taste.
6. Sprinkle with chopped fresh parsley and serve immediately with crusty bread for dipping.

Warm Hospitality Completes the Experience

The true magic of a seafood feast at a seaside konoba lies not just in the delicious food, but also in the warm hospitality. The attentive staff ensures your every need is met, offering recommendations and sharing stories about the local fishing traditions. As you savor the last bite, you'll feel a sense of connection to the place and its people, a feeling that resonates throughout your Montenegrin adventure.

A Journey for the Taste Buds

Exploring the world of Montenegrin seafood is a journey for the taste buds. From the simple elegance of grilled fish to the rich flavors of black risotto and mussels buzara every bite is an ode to the freshness of the Adriatic Sea and the culinary heritage of the country. Whether you're a seasoned seafood connoisseur or simply seeking a delicious and authentic dining experience, Montenegro offers a bounty of flavors waiting to be discovered.

Beyond the Konoba: Exploring Local Markets

While seaside konobas offer a delightful culinary experience, venturing into local markets allows you to delve deeper into the world of Montenegrin seafood. Imagine bustling stalls overflowing with glistening fish, plump mussels, and vibrant octopus. Engage with the friendly vendors, their faces weathered by years spent at sea, as they share their knowledge of the day's catch. Perhaps you'll pick up fresh ingredients to prepare your own seafood feast at a rented vacation villa, savoring the flavors in a more intimate setting.

Exploring local seafood markets resonates with the overall experience of exploring Montenegro. Just like embarking on a hike through a national park and encountering the diverse flora and fauna, visiting a local market allows you to connect with the source of the ingredients that grace Montenegrin tables. Imagine contrasting your market visit with a cooking class, where you can learn the secrets of preparing traditional seafood dishes from a local chef.

The culinary traditions surrounding Montenegrin seafood are a legacy passed down through generations. Fishing villages along the coast have for centuries relied on the bounty of the Adriatic to sustain them. The simplicity of the dishes, often featuring fresh catches cooked with local herbs and olive oil, reflects this deep connection to the sea. Every bite tells a story of resilience, tradition, and a deep respect for nature's bounty.

The flavors of Montenegrin seafood will leave a lasting impression long after your return home. The memory of succulent grilled fish, the rich aroma of mussels buzara, and the vibrant atmosphere of a seaside konoba will linger on your palate and in your heart. So, pack your bags and an adventurous spirit, and get ready to embark on a culinary journey through the captivating world of Montenegrin seafood.

Planning Your Seafood Adventure

Here are some additional tips for planning your seafood adventure in Montenegro:

- **Seasonal Specialties:** Certain seafood dishes are best enjoyed during specific seasons. For example, sea bass is at its peak in the summer, while spider crab is a winter delicacy.

- **Freshness is Key:** Look for restaurants and markets that display fresh catches daily. The glistening eyes and firm flesh of the fish are good indicators of freshness.

- **Embrace Local Specialties:** Don't be afraid to try unfamiliar dishes. Black risotto, mussels buzara, and grilled squid are all excellent choices for adventurous palates.

- **Learn a Few Phrases:** A few basic Montenegrin phrases like "ukusno" (delicious) and "hvala" (thank you) will go a long way in enhancing your dining experience.

A World of Flavor Awaits

Montenegro's coastline beckons you to savor its bounty of fresh seafood. From bustling markets overflowing with glistening catches to charming seaside konobas offering unforgettable culinary experiences, this captivating country promises a journey for your taste buds. So, pack your bags, an adventurous spirit, and an appetite for fresh flavors, and get ready to discover the magic of Montenegrin seafood.

Savoring Local Specialties (Gulaš, Pršut, Kačamak)

As you venture beyond the shimmering coastline and delve into the heart of Montenegro's dramatic mountains, a different kind of culinary adventure awaits. Here, hearty stews simmer in traditional pots, air-dried meats hang in cool cellars, and the comforting warmth of cornmeal mush fuels the lives of those who call these rugged landscapes home. Join us as we explore the world of Montenegrin mountain cuisine, a symphony of flavors that resonates with the country's rich heritage and the spirit of its mountain people.

A Tale of Two Gulašes: A Regional Culinary Journey

Gulaš (pronounced goo-lash), a rich stew simmered to perfection, is a cornerstone of Montenegrin mountain cuisine. But just like the diverse landscapes that define this country, there's no single version of this hearty dish. Imagine traveling from village to village, experiencing the subtle variations in each region's signature gulaš.

Northern Heariness

In the north, bordering Bosnia and Herzegovina, gulaš reflects the region's colder climate and heartier influences. Here, the stew is typically made with beef or lamb, slow-cooked with potatoes, carrots, onions, and a generous amount of paprika, resulting in a thick, deeply flavorful concoction. Cabbage or sauerkraut might be added for a touch of acidity, perfectly balancing the richness of the meat. This hearty gulaš is a true winter warmer, ideal for refueling after a day exploring the dramatic peaks of Durmitor National Park.

Coastal Influence in the South

As you travel south towards the Adriatic coast, the influence of the sea begins to permeate even the mountain cuisine. Here, gulaš might feature seafood alongside the traditional meat. Imagine a steaming bowl filled with tender chunks of octopus, mussels, or calamari simmered in a rich tomato sauce with potatoes, onions, and peppers. This lighter version of gulaš is a delightful contrast to its northern counterpart, a reminder of the diverse culinary influences that shape Montenegrin cuisine.

Resonating with the Hinterland

Savoring regional variations of gulaš resonates with the overall experience of exploring Montenegro's hinterland. Just like driving through charming villages lay close amidst rolling hills and vineyards, indulging in different gulašes offers a glimpse into the unique culinary traditions of each region. Imagine contrasting your hearty northern gulaš with a visit to a local winery, where you can sample delicious Montenegrin wines produced from grapes grown in the very valleys where this variation of the stew originated.

Beyond the Stew: A Celebration of Local Specialties

While gulaš might be the star of the show, Montenegrin mountain cuisine offers a bounty of other local specialties waiting to be discovered.

Pršut: A Savory Legacy

Pršut (pronounced proo-shoot), air-dried ham, is a Montenegrin delicacy with a long and storied history. Imagine venturing into a cool, dimly lit cellar, where rows of glistening pršut hang from the ceiling, the air thick with the intoxicating aroma of salt and spices. The traditional preparation process involves air-drying pork leg seasoned with salt and local herbs, resulting in a salty, savory ham that melts in your mouth. Pršut is often served thinly sliced as an appetizer, accompanied by crusty bread, strong cheese, and a glass of local red wine.

Kačamak: Comforting Simplicity

Kačamak (pronounced ka-cha-mak) is a simple yet comforting dish that has sustained generations of Montenegrin mountain people. Imagine a steaming bowl of creamy polenta made from cornmeal, traditionally cooked in a pot over an open fire. Kačamak can be enjoyed on its own or dressed up with cheese, butter, or even crumbled pršut for added richness. This versatile dish is a testament to the resourcefulness of the mountain people, using simple ingredients to create a satisfying and nutritious meal.

A Legacy of Resourcefulness

The focus on hearty stews, air-dried meats, and simple cornmeal dishes reflects the resourcefulness of the Montenegrin mountain people. Living in a region with harsh winters and limited agricultural land, they have learned to utilize local ingredients to create delicious and nourishing meals. Every bite of pršut or spoonful of kačamak tells a story of resilience and a deep respect for the bounty that the mountains provide.

A Lasting Impression

The flavors of Montenegrin mountain cuisine will leave a lasting impression long after your return home. The memory of a steaming bowl of hearty gulaš, the melt-in-your-mouth savoriness of pršut, and the comforting warmth of kačamak will linger on your palate and in your heart.

Montenegrin Pastries and Desserts

After exploring the diverse landscapes of Montenegro, from the sun-drenched coastline to the dramatic mountains, your taste buds deserve a sweet reward. This captivating country boasts a delectable array of pastries and desserts, each with a unique story to tell. Imagine indulging in warm, fluffy palačinke filled with sweet or savory goodness, or savoring a slice of krepschta, a layered pastry steeped in tradition. Join us as we delve into the world of Montenegrin sweets, a symphony of flavors that resonates with the country's rich heritage and the joy of sharing a delicious treat.

Palačinke: A Versatile Delight

Palačinke (pronounced pa-la-chin-keh) are the Montenegrin answer to the crepe. These thin pancakes are incredibly versatile, lending themselves to both sweet and savory fillings. Imagine the aroma of freshly baked palačinke filling the air as you settle into a cozy cafe. Perhaps you'll opt for the classic combination – a warm palačinke filled with a generous dollop of sweet, creamy Nutella. Or, for a more adventurous twist, you might choose a savory filling like cheese and ham, a delicious and satisfying option for lunch or a light dinner.

A Step-by-Step Guide to Making Palačinke

Creating your own palačinke at home is a delightful way to experience the magic of Montenegrin sweets. Here's a simple step-by-step guide:

Ingredients

- 2 cups (240g) all-purpose flour
- 3 large eggs
- 1 1/2 cups (350ml) milk

- 1 cup (240ml) water
- 1/4 teaspoon salt
- 2 tablespoons (30ml) melted butter

Instructions

1. In a large bowl, whisk together the flour, eggs, and salt. Gradually whisk in the milk and water until a smooth batter forms. Let the batter rest for at least 30 minutes.
2. Heat a non-stick pan or griddle over medium heat. Brush the pan with melted butter.
3. Pour about 1/4 cup of batter into the pan, swirling the pan to coat the bottom evenly.
4. Cook for about 1 minute per side, or until golden brown.
5. Repeat with remaining batter, adding more butter to the pan as needed.
6. Fill your palačinke with your desired filling. For sweet options, consider Nutella, jam, fresh fruit, or whipped cream. For savory fillings, try cheese and ham, roasted vegetables, or a creamy mushroom sauce.

Resonating with Fresh Flavors

Making your own palačinke resonates with the overall experience of exploring Montenegro. Just like visiting a local farmer's market and picking up fresh fruits and vegetables, preparing this dish allows you to connect with the ingredients that are central to Montenegrin cuisine. Imagine contrasting your palačinke-making experience with a visit to a beekeeping farm, where you can learn about the production of honey, a natural sweetener that often finds its way into fillings.

Krepschta: A Layered Legacy

Krepschta (pronounced krep-shta) is a layered pastry that holds a special place in Montenegrin culture. This rich dessert is traditionally served during festive occasions like weddings and holidays. Imagine a beautiful layered cake, flaky and golden brown from the outside, revealing a moist and flavorful interior of walnuts, poppy seeds, honey, and sometimes even dried fruit.

The Significance of Layers

The many layers of krepschta hold a symbolic significance. They represent the richness and complexity of Montenegrin culture, a drape woven from different influences. The act of sharing a slice of krepschta is a way of coming together and celebrating community.

A Legacy Passed Down Through Generations

The tradition of making krepschta is often passed down through generations, with each family having its own unique recipe. The preparation process can be time-consuming, but the reward is a delectable dessert that embodies the love and care poured into its creation. Every bite of krepschta tells a story of family traditions, cultural heritage, and the joy of sharing something special with loved ones.

A Lasting Impression

The sweetness of Montenegrin pastries and desserts will leave a lasting impression long after your return home. The memory of fluffy palačinke filled with your favorite flavor, the intricate layers of a celebratory krepschta, and the warmth of sharing these treats with friends and family will linger on your palate and in your heart.

Part 4: Practical Planning
ESSENTIAL INFORMATION FOR YOUR MONTENEGRIN ADVENTURE

Visas and Currency Exchange

As you gear up for your unforgettable adventure in Montenegro, a few practicalities need to be addressed to ensure a smooth and enjoyable experience. This chapter will guide you through the visa requirements and currency exchange considerations, allowing you to focus on the exciting experiences that await in this captivating Balkan nation.

Planning Your Visa: A Seamless Journey

The first step is understanding the visa requirements for entering Montenegro. The good news is that Montenegro boasts a visa-friendly approach, aligning closely with the Schengen Area. Imagine a seamless transition from planning your trip to exploring the wonders of Montenegro, thanks to a relaxed visa policy for many nationalities.

Visa-Free Entry for Many

A large portion of the world enjoys visa-free entry to Montenegro. Citizens of Schengen Area countries, with the exception of a few nations, can simply enter Montenegro with a valid passport. Additionally, several other countries, including Azerbaijan, Belarus, Kazakhstan, Russia, and Turkey, are granted visa-free entry for stays up to 90 days within a six-month period.

Double-Check for Exceptions

It's important to double-check the specific visa requirements for your nationality before finalizing your travel plans. Reliable resources like the official Montenegrin government website (https://travel.state.gov/content/travel/en/international-travel/International-Travel-Country-Information-Pages/Montenegro.html) or your local Montenegrin embassy or consulate can provide the most up-to-date information. They can also advise on any visa applications that might be necessary for your specific situation.

Visa Applications: A Streamlined Process

For those nationalities that do require a visa, the application process is generally streamlined. In most cases, you'll need to submit a completed application form, a valid passport, passport-sized photos, proof of travel insurance, and documentation of your planned accommodation and return flights. Visa processing times can vary, so factor this in when planning your trip.

Resonating with Efficiency

A smooth visa application process resonates with the overall experience of exploring Montenegro. Just like navigating the well-maintained roads that wind through beautiful landscapes, a streamlined visa process allows you to focus on the adventure that awaits. Imagine contrasting your efficient visa application with researching the best route for a scenic road trip through Montenegro, ensuring a seamless journey from planning to execution.

Currency Exchange: Essential Tips

Once your visa is secured, it's time to consider currency exchange. The official currency of Montenegro is the Euro, eliminating the need for complex currency conversions. This simplifies budgeting and spending during your trip.

Exchanging Your Cash

For those traveling from countries with a different currency, several options are available for exchanging your cash for Euros. Here are some tips to ensure you get the best possible exchange rate:

- **Exchange at Local Banks:** Banks in Montenegro typically offer competitive exchange rates. Look for banks with branches conveniently located near your arrival airport or accommodation.
- **Avoid Airport Kiosks:** While convenient, airport currency exchange kiosks often charge higher fees and offer less favorable exchange rates.
- **Consider Debit Cards:** Using your debit card to withdraw cash from ATMs in Montenegro can be a convenient option. However, be aware of any withdrawal fees that your bank might charge.

Planning Your Budget

Montenegro offers a range of travel experiences to suit all budgets. From budget-friendly guesthouses to luxurious beachfront resorts, there's something for everyone. Do some research on typical costs for accommodation, dining, activities, and transportation to establish a realistic budget for your trip.

A Resonant Experience

Managing your currency exchange effectively resonates with the overall experience of exploring Montenegro. Just like discovering hidden gems off the beaten path, finding ways to save money during your trip allows you to stretch your budget further and experience more of this captivating country. Imagine contrasting your research on favorable exchange rates with seeking out local restaurants serving delicious and affordable Montenegrin cuisine.

The Adventure Begins

With the visa requirements addressed and your currency exchange sorted, you're now well-equipped to embark on your Montenegrin adventure. The following chapters will delve deeper into the practicalities of planning your trip, from finding the perfect accommodation to navigating transportation options. So, pack your bags, a sense of adventure, and get ready to discover the magic of Montenegro!

Getting There and Getting Around: Transportation Options in Montenegro

The anticipation builds as you embark on your journey to Montenegro. This captivating Balkan nation awaits, beckoning you to explore its dramatic coastlines, majestic mountains, and charming villages. But before you can indulge in the country's delectable cuisine and rich cultural heritage, you need to consider the various ways to reach this Adriatic gem. This chapter will guide you through the different transportation options available, allowing you to choose the one that best resonates with your travel style and itinerary.

Taking Flight: Soaring Towards Adventure

For many travelers, reaching Montenegro by air is the most convenient and time-efficient option. Two main airports serve the country, each offering a unique gateway to different regions:

- **Tivat Airport:** Lay close on the stunning Bay of Kotor, Tivat Airport is a popular choice for those seeking a coastal escape. Imagine stepping off the plane and being greeted by breathtaking views of turquoise waters and dramatic mountains, instantly setting the stage for your Montenegrin adventure. This airport primarily handles seasonal charter flights and flights from major European cities.
- **Podgorica Airport:** As Montenegro's capital city, Podgorica boasts the country's largest airport. This hub offers year-round connections to major European destinations, making it a good choice for travelers seeking

flexibility and a wider range of flight options. From Podgorica, you can easily connect to other parts of Montenegro by bus, train, or rental car.

Resonating with Your Itinerary

Choosing your arrival airport should resonate with your overall itinerary. Imagine planning your trip around specific destinations. If your dream vacation involves exploring the charming coastal towns of Budva, Kotor, and Herceg Novi, then Tivat Airport might be the ideal entry point. On the other hand, if you're planning to delve deeper into the heart of Montenegro and explore historic towns like Cetinje and Nikšić, Podgorica Airport might be a more convenient option.

A Seafaring Adventure: Sailing into Montenegro

For those seeking a more adventurous and scenic approach, reaching Montenegro by ferry is a captivating option. Imagine the salty breeze whipping through your hair as you cruise across the sparkling Adriatic Sea, savoring the anticipation of your Montenegrin adventure. Ferry services connect Montenegro with neighboring countries, offering a unique way to arrive:

- **Ferries from Croatia:** Regular ferry services operate between Dubrovnik, Croatia, and Kotor, Montenegro. This scenic journey allows you to experience two captivating Balkan countries in one trip. Imagine departing from the historic city walls of Dubrovnik and arriving in the heart of Montenegro's dramatic Bay of Kotor, a UNESCO World Heritage Site.

- **Ferries from Italy:** For those traveling from Italy, ferry connections operate between Bari, Italy, and Bar, Montenegro. This longer journey offers a chance to relax and enjoy the seafaring experience. Imagine gazing out at the endless blue horizon, the anticipation building as you approach the rugged Montenegrin coastline.

Resonating with Your Travel Style

Choosing to arrive by ferry resonates with your overall travel style. If you crave a unique and scenic journey, then sailing into Montenegro might be the perfect choice. Imagine contrasting your ferry experience with exploring the charming coastal towns along the Bay of Kotor, each with its own distinct character and historical charm. The ferry journey becomes an extension of your adventure, offering a glimpse of the Adriatic's beauty before you set foot on Montenegrin soil.

Navigating the Land: Getting Around Montenegro

Once you've arrived in Montenegro, a variety of transportation options await to help you explore the country's diverse landscapes:

- **Car Rentals:** Renting a car offers the ultimate flexibility and freedom to explore Montenegro at your own pace. Imagine venturing off the beaten path, discovering hidden villages lay close amidst rolling hills, and stopping at scenic viewpoints along the way. A rental car allows you to create your own personalized itinerary and truly immerse yourself in the beauty of Montenegro.

- **Buses:** Montenegro's well-maintained bus network connects most major towns and cities. This is a budget-friendly option for getting around, especially if you're traveling on a tight budget. While timetables might not be as frequent as in other European countries, buses offer a chance to interact with locals and experience the rhythm of daily life in Montenegro.

- **Trains:** The Montenegrin railway system is limited but offers a scenic journey through the country's dramatic landscapes. The most popular route is the Belgrade-Bar railway, which winds its way through canyons and mountains, offering breathtaking views. Taking the train is a unique way to experience the Montenegrin countryside and connect with fellow travelers.

Resonating with Your Exploration Style

Choosing your mode of transportation resonates with your exploration style. Imagine contrasting the freedom of a rental car, allowing you to discover hidden beaches and charming villages at your own whim, with the laid-back charm of a train journey. As the train snakes through dramatic canyons and verdant valleys, you can sit back, relax, and soak in the Montenegrin scenery. This resonates with a slower pace of travel, allowing you to truly appreciate the beauty of the landscape.

Local Taxis: Taxis are readily available in major towns and cities, offering a convenient way to get around, particularly for short distances or late-night travel. However, fares can be higher compared to buses, so it's best to agree on a price before getting in. Taxis can be a good option for day trips to nearby villages or excursions outside of the main public transportation routes.

Ridesharing Apps: While not as widespread as in other countries, ridesharing apps are becoming increasingly popular in Montenegro, particularly in major cities like Podgorica and Budva. This can be a convenient and affordable way to get around, especially if you're traveling with a group and want to share the cost.

Choosing Your Mode of Transport

The best mode of transport for you depends on your travel style, budget, and itinerary. Here are some factors to consider when making your decision:

- **Flexibility:** For maximum flexibility and freedom to explore at your own pace, a rental car is the ideal choice.

- **Budget:** Buses are the most budget-friendly option, while taxis and ridesharing apps can be more expensive.
- **Time:** If you're short on time, flying is the quickest way to reach Montenegro. However, exploring by bus or train allows you to see more of the countryside.
- **Experience:** For a unique and scenic journey, consider arriving by ferry or taking the Belgrade-Bar railway.

The way you choose to get around Montenegro resonates with the overall experience of exploring this captivating country. Just like savoring the diverse flavors of Montenegrin cuisine, from fresh seafood to hearty stews, each mode of transport offers a unique way to connect with the landscape, culture, and people. Imagine contrasting the freedom of a road trip with the camaraderie of a train journey, each adding a distinct layer to your Montenegrin adventure.

With your transportation options explored, you're now well-equipped to navigate the captivating landscapes of Montenegro. The following chapters will delve deeper into planning your itinerary, from finding the perfect accommodation to choosing must-see attractions and activities. So, buckle up, lace up your walking shoes, and get ready to discover the magic of Montenegro, one adventure at a time!

Choosing Your Transport

Montenegro, a Balkan gem, beckons with its dramatic coastline, majestic mountains, and charming villages. Planning your transportation is crucial for unlocking the country's diverse beauty. Should you explore with the freedom of a rental car, navigate by budget-friendly bus, or rely on the convenience of taxis? This guide will explore the pros and cons of each option, empowering you to choose the transportation style that resonates with your travel desires.

The Freedom of the Open Road: Renting a Car

Imagine cruising along the scenic coastal route, stopping at hidden coves for a refreshing swim, and venturing off the beaten path to discover quaint villages. Renting a car offers unparalleled flexibility and control over your itinerary.

Pros

- **Freedom and Flexibility:** A rental car grants you the freedom to explore at your own pace, creating a personalized itinerary that suits your interests. Detour to breathtaking viewpoints, discover hidden gems, and adjust your schedule as you wish.

- **Off-the-Beaten-Path Exploration:** Public transportation might not reach every corner of Montenegro. A car allows you to access remote areas, charming villages tucked away in valleys, and hidden beaches accessible only by dirt roads.

- **Luggage and Gear:** Traveling with bulky luggage or sporting equipment becomes easier with a car. No need to worry about lugging your bags on and off buses or fitting them into taxis.

Cons

- **Cost:** Renting a car can be the most expensive option, especially considering fuel costs and potential one-way drop-off fees. Factor in insurance and parking costs as well.

- **Navigation Challenges:** Montenegro's road network can be a maze of winding roads and unclear signage. Invest in a reliable GPS or download offline maps to navigate confidently.

- **Parking Woes:** Finding parking in popular tourist destinations, especially during peak season, can be a challenge. Be prepared for limited parking options and potential fees.

Ideal for

Travelers seeking an independent adventure, those exploring remote areas, groups splitting the cost, and those with bulky luggage or sporting equipment.

The Budget-Friendly Explorer: Public Buses

Imagine the rhythmic thrum of the engine as you journey through the Montenegrin countryside, sharing the experience with locals and fellow travelers. Bus travel offers a budget-friendly option for exploring major towns and cities.

Pros

- **Cost-Effective:** Buses are the most affordable way to get around Montenegro. Tickets are inexpensive, allowing you to stretch your travel budget further.

- **Relaxation and Scenery:** Sit back, relax, and let the driver handle the navigation. Enjoy the scenic vistas unfolding through the window, soaking in the changing landscapes.

- **Social Interaction:** Bus travel offers a chance to interact with locals and fellow travelers. Strike up conversations, learn about local culture, and gain travel tips from seasoned explorers.

Cons

- **Limited Flexibility:** Bus schedules dictate your itinerary. You might have to wait for connections or adjust your plans around bus timings. Limited stops and fixed routes restrict your ability to explore off-the-beaten-path locations.

- **Time Constraints:** Bus travel can be slower than a rental car, especially with multiple stops and potential delays. Factor in travel time when planning your itinerary.
- **Luggage Logistics:** Managing bulky luggage can be inconvenient on crowded buses. Be prepared to carry your bags on and off the bus, and consider packing light.

Ideal for

Budget-conscious travelers, those comfortable with fixed schedules, solo adventurers seeking social interaction, and those with minimal luggage.

The Convenience Factor: Relying on Taxis

Imagine hailing a taxi for a comfortable ride to your hotel after a long flight, or flagging one down for a spontaneous day trip to a nearby town. Taxis offer convenience, especially for short distances or late-night travel.

Pros

- **Convenience:** Taxis are readily available in major towns and cities, offering a quick and comfortable way to get around, especially for short distances or late-night trips. No need to worry about schedules or navigating unfamiliar roads.
- **Door-to-Door Service:** The ease of being dropped off right at your doorstep or desired location is unmatched. No lugging your luggage on long walks or navigating public transport in unfamiliar areas.
- **Spontaneous Exploration:** Taxis offer flexibility for spontaneous day trips or exploring nightlife options without relying on public transportation schedules.

Cons

- **Cost:** Taxis are the most expensive option compared to buses or renting a car, especially for longer distances. Agree on a fare beforehand to avoid surprises.
- **Limited Availability:** Taxis might be scarce in smaller villages or remote areas. Relying solely on taxis might limit your exploration options, especially outside major towns and cities.
- **Language Barrier:** Communication with taxi drivers can be a challenge if you don't speak Montenegrin. Having basic phrases or a translation app handy can be helpful.

Ideal for

Travelers with limited mobility or heavy luggage, those arriving late at night or departing early in the morning, short-distance trips within cities, and those comfortable with potentially higher costs for the convenience.

The Perfect Choice Awaits

The ideal transportation option for your Montenegrin adventure hinges on your travel style, budget, and itinerary. Consider these factors when making your decision:

- **Budget:** Buses offer the most budget-friendly option, while taxis can be the most expensive. Rental cars fall somewhere in between, depending on fuel costs and car size.
- **Flexibility:** Rental cars offer the most freedom to explore at your own pace, while buses and taxis have limitations due to schedules and availability.

- **Itinerary:** Are you sticking to major towns, or venturing off-the-beaten-path? Buses connect major destinations, while cars and taxis offer access to remote areas.

- **Luggage:** Traveling light makes buses and taxis more manageable. Rental cars are ideal for those with bulky luggage or sporting equipment.

- **Comfort and Convenience:** Taxis offer the most comfortable and convenient option, especially for short distances or late-night travel.

The way you choose to navigate Montenegro becomes an extension of your travel style. Imagine contrasting the budget-conscious spirit of bus travel with the luxurious comfort of a taxi ride. Each option allows you to experience Montenegro from a different perspective. Bus travel immerses you in the local rhythm, while a rental car grants you the freedom to explore at your own whim.

Ultimately, the best transportation option is the one that allows you to create unforgettable memories in Montenegro. Whether you cruise along the coast in a rental car, soak in the scenery on a budget-friendly bus ride, or hail a taxi for a spontaneous adventure, your choice will resonate with your unique travel desires. So, pack your bags, choose your transport mode, and get ready to discover the magic of Montenegro!

Finding Your Perfect Accommodation: From Budget Hostels to Luxury Resorts

Landing in Montenegro is just the beginning of your captivating adventure. Now it's time to find your home away from home, a place that reflects your travel style and complements your exploration plans. From budget-friendly hostels bustling with fellow adventurers to luxurious resorts offering unparalleled pampering, Montenegro caters to every traveler's desire.

Immersing Yourself in Local Charm: Guesthouses and Boutique Hotels

For those seeking an authentic Montenegrin experience, guesthouses and boutique hotels offer a unique blend of charm and comfort. Imagine staying in a lovingly restored stone building in a charming village, or a tastefully decorated hotel lay close amidst vineyards. These smaller establishments often boast personal touches and a connection to the local community.

Guesthouses

1. **Prženović Guesthouse (Bay of Kotor):** Lay close in the heart of the UNESCO World Heritage Site, this family-run guesthouse offers breathtaking views of the Bay of Kotor and a warm welcome. (Booking.com, starts from €40 per night, traditional Montenegrin hospitality, breathtaking bay views)

2. **Villa Milica (Sveti Stefan):** This charming guesthouse on the prestigious Sveti Stefan peninsula boasts stunning sea views and a relaxed atmosphere. (Website: https://www.airbnb.com/rooms/50541310, starts from €80 per night, peaceful setting close to the beach, ideal for couples)

3. **Dragsanović Guest House (Virpazar):** This traditional Montenegrin guesthouse, located in the heart of the Skadar Lake National Park, offers a unique opportunity to experience local culture and stunning natural beauty. (Booking.com, starts from €50 per night, traditional lakefront accommodation, boat tours available)

4. **Hijacinta House (Cetinje):** Step back in time at this historic guesthouse in Montenegro's former royal capital. Centrally located and beautifully decorated, it offers easy access to the city's cultural treasures. (Website: https://www.booking.com/hotel/me/stone-house-264.html, starts from €65 per night, historic charm in the heart of Cetinje, close to museums and palaces)

5. **Nikšić Heritage House (Nikšić):** Immerse yourself in Montenegrin history at this restored 19th-century stone house in Nikšić. The guesthouse offers a unique blend of traditional architecture and modern amenities. (Booking.com, starts from €70 per night, historic setting in Nikšić's old town, close to restaurants and shops)

6. **Lavender Bay Guesthouse (Herceg Novi):** This charming guesthouse in Herceg Novi boasts a beautiful garden and stunning sea views. Enjoy a relaxing stay close to the beach and explore the town's charming Old Town. (Website: https://www.booking.com/hotel/me/lavender-bay-d9.html, starts from €90 per night, tranquil location with sea views, perfect for relaxation)

7. **Vila Flora (Boko Bay):** Lay close amidst the lush greenery of Boko Bay, this family-run guesthouse offers a peaceful escape close to the historical town of Perast. (Booking.com, starts from €55 per night, family-friendly atmosphere, close to Perast and boat tours)

Boutique Hotels

1. **Hotel Hippocampus (Budva):** This stylish boutique hotel in Budva's Old Town offers a unique blend of modern design and historical charm. Enjoy stunning views of the Adriatic Sea and explore the vibrant coastal town. (Website: https://www.booking.com/hotel/me/hippocampus.html, starts from €120 per night, modern luxury in Budva's Old Town, perfect for exploring history and nightlife)

2. **Hotel Chetu (Sveti Stefan):** Experience contemporary luxury at this boutique hotel on the exclusive Sveti Stefan peninsula. Enjoy breathtaking sea views, infinity pools, and impeccable service. (Website: https://www.aman.com/resorts/aman-sveti-stefan, starts from €250 per night, luxurious retreat on Sveti Stefan, perfect for relaxation and indulgence)

3. **Hotel Lovcen (Kotor):** This charming boutique hotel in Kotor's Old Town offers a unique experience within the medieval city walls. Enjoy beautifully decorated rooms and a rooftop terrace with stunning views. (Website: https://www.booking.com/hotel/me/hostel-lovcen.sr.html, starts from €150 per night, historic charm in Kotor's Old Town, perfect for exploring the city)

4. **Boutique Hotel Astoria (Kotor):** This elegant hotel in Kotor's Old Town boasts stunning views of the Bay of Kotor and impeccable service. The hotel's rooftop restaurant offers a romantic dining experience. (starts from €180 per night, elegant setting in Kotor's Old Town, perfect for couples and romantic getaways)

5. **Hotel Fjords (Pržno):** Escape to a secluded paradise at this luxurious boutique hotel lay close on the shores of the Bay of Kotor. Enjoy private beach access, infinity pools, and

breathtaking sea views. (Website: [invalid URL removed], starts from €200 per night, secluded luxury on the Bay of Kotor, perfect for relaxation and rejuvenation)
6. **Villa Duomo (Sveti Stefan):** This elegant boutique hotel on the prestigious Sveti Stefan peninsula offers stunning sea views, an outdoor pool, and a spa. Enjoy a luxurious retreat close to the charming island village. (Website: [https://www.villaduomo.com])

Budget-Friendly Options: Hostels and Apartments

For the budget-conscious traveler or those planning an extended stay, Montenegro offers a range of hostels and apartments that provide comfortable and affordable accommodation. Imagine being at the heart of the action in a social hostel setting, connecting with fellow adventurers and sharing travel stories. Apartments, on the other hand, offer a more independent living experience, allowing you to cook your own meals and feel at home away from home.

Finding Hostels and Apartments

Several online platforms can help you find budget-friendly accommodation in Montenegro. Here are a few popular options:

- **Hostelworld:** (https://www.hostelworld.com/) - A leading platform for finding hostels worldwide, offering a wide range of options in Montenegro with detailed descriptions, reviews, and secure booking.

- **Booking.com:** (https://www.booking.com/) - While not solely focused on budget stays, Booking.com offers a good selection of hostels and apartments in Montenegro, with user reviews and clear pricing information.

- **Airbnb:** (https://www.airbnb.com/) - This popular platform allows you to find unique apartments and homestays in

Montenegro, offering a chance to experience local culture and live like a resident.

Top 10 Budget-Friendly Options

Hostels

1. **Old Town Hostel Kotor:** Situated within Kotor's Old Town walls, this social hostel offers dorm beds, private rooms, and a rooftop terrace with stunning views. (Starts from €15 per night on Hostelworld)

2. **Montenegro Backpacker Hostel (Budva):** This social hostel in the heart of Budva offers a lively atmosphere, comfortable dorm beds, and a rooftop bar with sea views. (Starts from €18 per night on Booking.com)

3. **Wanderlust Hostel (Sveti Stefan):** This laid-back hostel near Sveti Stefan boasts a swimming pool, a garden, and a shared kitchen. Perfect for socializing and exploring the stunning coastline. (Starts from €20 per night on Airbnb)

4. **Hostel 212 (Podgorica):** This modern hostel in Montenegro's capital offers comfortable dorm beds, a shared kitchen, and a common area for socializing. (Starts from €12 per night on Hostelworld)

5. **Happy Hours Hostel (Bar):** This social hostel in Bar, Montenegro's southern coastal town, offers dorm beds, private rooms, and a rooftop terrace with sea views. (Starts from €17 per night on Booking.com)

Apartments

1. **Cozy Kotor Bay Apartment:** This charming one-bedroom apartment in Kotor offers stunning bay views and a central location for exploring the Old Town. (Starts from €40 per night on Airbnb)

2. **Budva Sea View Apartment:** This modern two-bedroom apartment in Budva boasts a balcony with sea views and a short walk to the beach. (Starts from €50 per night on Booking.com)

3. **Lake Skadar Apartment:** This one-bedroom apartment in Virpazar, on the shores of Lake Skadar, offers a peaceful setting close to nature and boat tours. (Starts from €35 per night on Airbnb)

4. **Nikšić Old Town Apartment:** This cozy studio apartment in Nikšić's Old Town provides a comfortable base for exploring the historic city center. (Starts from €45 per night on Booking.com)

5. **Boko Bay Apartment:** This two-bedroom apartment in Herceg Novi offers sea views, a balcony, and a convenient location close to shops and restaurants. (Starts from €60 per night on Airbnb)

Tips for Booking Budget Accommodation

- **Book in Advance:** Especially during peak season (July and August), popular hostels and apartments can fill up quickly. Booking in advance ensures you secure your desired accommodation.

- **Consider Location:** While central locations offer convenience, slightly further out options might be more affordable. Factor in walking distances or public transportation costs when making your decision.

- **Read Reviews:** Reviews from previous guests offer valuable insights into the hostel or apartment's atmosphere, amenities, and cleanliness.

- **Look for Deals and Discounts:** Many hostels and apartments offer special deals or discounts for longer stays or last-minute bookings.

Resonating with Your Travel Style

Choosing between a hostel or apartment ultimately resonates with your travel style. Imagine the camaraderie and social interaction of a hostel setting, perfect for meeting fellow travelers and sharing experiences. Apartments, on the other hand, offer privacy, a sense of home, and the flexibility to cook your own meals and set your own schedule.

Your Montenegrin Adventure Awaits

With a wide range of accommodation options available, you're now well-equipped to find the perfect place to rest your head during your Montenegrin adventure. Whether you choose a charming guesthouse steeped in local charm, a luxurious boutique

Packing Essentials for All Seasons and Activities

Your bags are practically packed, your transportation secured, and your accommodation awaits. But before you embark on your Montenegrin adventure, it's crucial to ensure you've packed the essentials for the season and activities you have planned. Imagine navigating the bustling coastal towns in summer attire, or conquering snowy peaks with the proper winter gear. This chapter will guide you through creating a packing list that resonates with your planned adventures, ensuring you're prepared for anything Montenegro throws your way.

Summer Delights: Packing for Sun-Kissed Adventures

Montenegro's summer beckons with its dazzling coastline, shimmering turquoise waters, and vibrant coastal towns. As you pack for your sun-kissed adventure, here are some essential items to ensure comfort and preparedness:

- **Sun Protection:** Pack high-factor sunscreen (SPF 30 or higher) to shield your skin from the strong Mediterranean sun. Don't forget a hat with a wide brim to protect your face and neck, and sunglasses to safeguard your eyes.

- **Beach Essentials:** Pack several swimsuits to cater to your swimming adventures. Quick-drying towels will come in handy for beach lounging or poolside relaxation. Consider including beach sandals or flip-flops for easy on-and-off access to the water.

- **Comfortable Clothing:** Breathable fabrics like cotton or linen are ideal for staying cool in the summer heat. Pack lightweight shirts, shorts, skirts, and comfortable dresses for exploring towns and soaking up the sunshine. A light sweater or scarf can be handy for cooler evenings.

- **Walking Shoes:** Comfortable walking shoes are a must for navigating cobbled streets, exploring charming villages, and venturing off the beaten path. While sandals offer a breezy option, consider shoes with good ankle support for uneven terrain.

- **Quick-Drying Clothing:** If you plan on participating in water activities like kayaking or boat tours, pack a quick-drying shirt and shorts or a lightweight rashguard. These will ensure you stay comfortable after your aquatic adventure.

- **Essentials for the Evening:** Pack a light outfit for evenings out, whether it's a casual dinner at a seaside restaurant or exploring the nightlife in Budva or Kotor. Don't forget a light jacket or wrap for cooler coastal breezes.

Resonating with Your Activities

Remember, your packing list should resonate with your planned activities. If you're a hiking enthusiast, consider packing a pair of lightweight hiking boots for exploring Montenegro's many trails. For those planning on attending cultural events or upscale restaurants, pack one dressier outfit for those special occasions.

Winter Wonderland: Packing for Montenegrin Mountains

Montenegro transforms into a winter wonderland during the colder months, offering stunning snow-capped peaks, charming ski resorts, and opportunities for winter sports. Packing for winter adventures requires a different approach:

- **Warm Layers:** Pack thermals, fleece jackets, and a warm winter coat to ensure you stay toasty in the cooler temperatures. Layering allows you to adjust to changing weather conditions throughout the day.
- **Waterproof Gear:** A waterproof jacket and snow pants are essential for protecting yourself from snow and rain. Consider waterproof boots with good traction for navigating icy or snowy terrain.
- **Proper Footwear:** Invest in a good pair of winter boots with sturdy soles and good ankle support. These will be crucial for exploring snowy landscapes, navigating icy sidewalks, or venturing on winter hikes.
- **Winter Accessories:** Don't forget warm socks, gloves, a beanie, and a scarf to keep your extremities warm and cozy. Sunglasses are also important for protecting your eyes from the glare of the snow.
- **Ski Gear:** If you plan on hitting the slopes, pack your ski or snowboard gear, including appropriate clothing, boots,

poles, and any necessary accessories. Some ski resorts offer rentals, so check their website beforehand.

Resonating with Your Exploration Style

Packing for winter adventures in Montenegro resonates with your exploration style. For those planning on relaxing in ski resorts and enjoying après-ski activities, pack cozy loungewear and comfortable shoes for exploring the village. Hikers venturing into the snowy peaks will need to be more meticulous, ensuring they have all the necessary gear for safe and enjoyable winter exploration.

Packing for All Seasons

Montenegro offers a diverse range of experiences throughout the year. Here are some additional tips to ensure your packing list caters to all seasons:

- **Versatile Clothing:** Opt for neutral-colored clothing that can be easily mixed and matched, allowing you to create multiple outfits with fewer pieces.

- **Travel-Sized Toiletries:** Pack travel-sized toiletries to save space in your luggage. Many hotels provide basic toiletries as well.

- **Electronics and Chargers:** Don't forget to pack your chargers, adapters (Montenegro uses the standard European two round prong plug), and any necessary electronics like cameras, headphones, or a portable power bank to keep your devices charged during your adventures.

- **First-Aid Kit:** Pack a basic first-aid kit with essential medications like pain relievers, allergy medication, bandaids, and antiseptic wipes for minor cuts or scrapes.

- **Quick-Drying Laundry Bag:** A quick-drying laundry bag allows you to easily wash and dry smaller items while

- traveling, especially handy for longer stays or active itineraries.

- **Reusable Water Bottle:** Stay hydrated by bringing a reusable water bottle. Montenegro boasts clean tap water, so you can refill your bottle throughout the day and reduce plastic waste.

Beyond the Essentials: Personalizing Your Packing List

This guide provides a foundation for packing for your Montenegrin adventure. Remember to personalize your list based on your specific needs and interests. Here are some additional considerations:

- **Activities:** Are you planning any specific activities like hiking, biking, or kayaking? Pack appropriate gear for your chosen pursuits.

- **Dietary Restrictions:** If you have any dietary restrictions, pack some snacks or travel-friendly food items to ensure you have options readily available.

- **Entertainment:** Pack a book, travel journal, or download some movies or music to keep yourself entertained during downtime or travel days.

- **Personal Comfort Items:** Pack any items that enhance your personal comfort, such as an eye mask for sleeping on planes or trains, earplugs for noisy environments, or a small pillow for added comfort.

With a well-thought-out packing list, you're now prepared to embark on your Montenegrin adventure, ready for any season or activity you have planned. Imagine navigating the cobbled streets of Kotor with your comfortable walking shoes, or conquering snowy peaks with your trusty winter gear. Remember, packing goes beyond just clothes; it's about bringing the essentials that will make your journey comfortable, enjoyable, and allow you to create lasting memories in this captivating Balkan nation. So, pack your bags, embrace the spirit of adventure, and get ready to discover the magic of Montenegro!

MONTENEGRO BEYOND

Secret Beaches

Montenegro's coastline stretches like a painter's canvas, boasting dramatic cliffs, hidden coves, and dazzling turquoise waters. While the allure of popular beaches like Jaz or Sveti Stefan is undeniable, a true adventurer craves the hidden gems. Imagine discovering a secluded cove accessible only by boat, a pristine sanctuary untouched by mass tourism. This chapter unveils the magic of Montenegro's secret beaches, offering a glimpse into a paradise waiting to be explored.

Unveiling a Secluded Paradise

Imagine a hidden cove lay close amidst rugged cliffs, accessible only by a short boat ride. As you approach, the turquoise water shimmers like a polished gem, reflecting the azure sky above. Fine, white pebbles line the shore, leading to a secluded stretch of pristine sand. The only sound is the gentle lapping of waves against the shore and the melodic calls of seabirds circling overhead. This is the magic of Montenegro's secret beaches – a haven of tranquility and an escape from the crowds.

Exploring the Untouched Sanctuary

Dipping your toes into the crystal-clear water, you're greeted by refreshing coolness. The water's clarity allows you to see the vibrant marine life swimming beneath the surface. With no sun loungers or beach umbrellas cluttering the landscape, the view is pristine, offering a sense of connection with the raw beauty of nature. Imagine snorkeling amidst colorful coral reefs, or simply stretching out on the warm sand with a book, basking in the tranquility of your secluded paradise.

A Haven for Adventure

Beyond sunbathing and swimming, these hidden coves offer opportunities for exploration. Imagine kayaking along the rugged coastline, discovering hidden caves and inlets inaccessible by land. For the adventurous soul, some coves offer challenging hikes down cliffs, leading to breathtaking viewpoints and secluded beaches. The possibilities are endless, and the reward is the discovery of a hidden gem that feels like your own personal sanctuary.

Responsible Tourism: Protecting Paradise

The allure of Montenegro's secret beaches comes with a responsibility – to protect these pristine environments for future generations. Here are some essential tips for practicing responsible tourism when exploring hidden coves:

- **Leave No Trace:** Pack out all your trash, including food scraps, plastic bottles, and cigarette butts. Dispose of waste responsibly in designated bins upon returning to the mainland.

- **Respect the Environment:** Avoid disturbing wildlife or plant life. Steer clear of sensitive areas and refrain from collecting shells or rocks, allowing the natural beauty to remain untouched.

- **Minimize Noise Pollution:** Respect the tranquility of the cove. Keep music levels low and avoid loud activities that may disrupt the peaceful atmosphere.

- **Support Local Communities:** If you hire a local boat operator to reach the cove, consider patronizing restaurants or shops run by local families upon your return.

By following these principles, you can ensure that these hidden gems remain pristine sanctuaries for generations to come. Imagine the satisfaction of contributing to the preservation of these natural wonders while enjoying their breathtaking beauty.

The exploration of secret beaches resonates with the overall spirit of adventure in Montenegro. Renting a car and following a dusty trail might lead you to a hidden cove, or chartering a local fisherman's boat might unlock a secluded paradise. The key is to embrace the sense of discovery and appreciate the unique experiences these hidden gems offer.

Montenegro's coastline is a treasure trove of hidden coves, each offering a unique experience. With careful exploration and responsible behavior, you can unlock the magic of these secret beaches, creating unforgettable memories in the process. So, pack your swimsuit, a sense of adventure, and a commitment to responsible tourism, and get ready to discover the hidden wonders of Montenegro's untouched coastline.

Charming Villages

Montenegro's allure extends far beyond its dazzling coastline. Lay close amidst dramatic mountains and rolling hills lie charming villages that embody the soul of the country. Imagine strolling through cobbled streets lined with stone houses, encountering friendly locals, and savoring a taste of authentic Montenegrin culture. This chapter takes you on a virtual walk through some of these hidden gems, offering a glimpse into the heart of Montenegro.

Njeguši: A Village Steeped in History

Our journey begins in Njeguši, a village perched on the slopes of Mount Lovćen, overlooking the Bay of Kotor. This village holds immense historical significance as the birthplace of Peter the Great, a ruler who modernized Russia in the 18th century. As you wander through Njeguši, time seems to slow down. Traditional stone houses with terracotta roofs line the narrow streets, adorned with vibrant flower pots and overflowing with character. Atop a hill stands the Mausoleum of Petar Petrović Njegoš, a revered Montenegrin poet and ruler, offering breathtaking panoramic views of the surrounding landscape. The village is also renowned for its production of smoked ham, "Njeguški pršut," a local delicacy cured in the fresh mountain air. Imagine indulging in a plate of this regional specialty at a family-run restaurant, savoring the smoky flavors while soaking in the historic ambiance.

Pržno: A Fishing Village with Tranquility

Our next stop is Pržno, a hidden gem lay close on the shores of the Maëstrada Bay. This charming fishing village exudes a sense of tranquility, a stark contrast to the vibrancy of Budva or Kotor. Imagine strolling along the picturesque harbor, lined with colorful fishing boats gently bobbing on the turquoise water. Quaint cafes and restaurants spill onto cobbled streets, tempting you with fresh seafood dishes and breathtaking sea views. Pržno boasts a beautiful beach with soft, golden sand, perfect for swimming, sunbathing, or simply relaxing with a good book. Venture further and explore the surrounding olive groves, or hike along scenic trails offering panoramic vistas of the coastline. Pržno's relaxed atmosphere and slower pace of life offer a welcome escape from the hustle and bustle of everyday life.

Virpazar: A Picturesque Escape on Skadar Lake

Leaving the coast behind, we head towards Virpazar, a picturesque town lay close on the banks of Lake Skadar, Montenegro's largest lake and a designated National Park. Imagine arriving by boat, taking in the beauty of the turquoise waters framed by lush green mountains. Virpazar boasts a charming harbor lined with traditional wooden houses and vibrant cafes. This town is a haven for nature lovers, offering boat tours through the serene waters of the lake, where you can spot a diverse range of birdlife, including pelicans, herons, and cormorants. Venture into the surrounding villages and experience authentic Montenegrin life, or explore the nearby historical sites like the ruins of the medieval fortress, Besac. Virpazar offers a unique blend of natural beauty, cultural richness, and a laid-back atmosphere, making it the perfect escape for the soul.

Beyond the Tourist Trail: Uncovering Hidden Gems

These are just a few examples of the many charming villages waiting to be discovered in Montenegro. For the intrepid traveler, venturing beyond the tourist trail can lead to hidden gems like:

- **Đinovići:** A small village located on the Luštica peninsula, offering a relaxed atmosphere, beautiful beaches, and stunning views of the Bay of Kotor.

- **Perast:** A UNESCO World Heritage Site boasting a unique collection of 17th and 18th-century churches lay close amidst a dramatic backdrop of mountains and overlooking the Bay of Kotor.

- **Rijeka Crnojevića:** A historic town lay close on the banks of the River Crnojevića, known for its Ottoman-era stone bridge and traditional architecture.

A Journey Through Time and Culture

Each village offers a glimpse into Montenegro's rich history and vibrant culture. Imagine engaging in conversation with local artisans selling their handcrafted souvenirs, or savoring a traditional Montenegrin meal prepared with fresh, local ingredients. These charming villages offer a distinct contrast to the coastal resorts, providing a more authentic and immersive experience.

Exploring Montenegro's charming villages resonates with the adventurous spirit. Renting a car and following scenic winding roads can lead you to unexpected discoveries. Alternatively, consider joining a guided tour that delves deeper into the history and culture of these hidden gems. The key is to embrace the sense of exploration and allow yourself to be captivated by the charm and beauty of these traditional villages.

Bargaining at Local Markets and Shopping for Souvenirs

Your Montenegrin adventure wouldn't be complete without immersing yourself in the vibrant atmosphere of local markets. Imagine strolling through colorful stalls overflowing with fresh produce, handcrafted souvenirs, and local delicacies. While the sights and smells are captivating, navigating the art of bargaining can be a fun and rewarding experience. This chapter equips you with the knowledge and cultural understanding to navigate local markets and return home with unique treasures that resonate with your memories.

The Thrill of the Hunt: Exploring Local Markets

Montenegro boasts a plethora of local markets, each offering a glimpse into the local way of life. From the bustling open-air markets in cities like Kotor and Budva to the charming farmers' markets in smaller villages, every corner holds the potential for discovery. Here are some tips for navigating these vibrant marketplaces:

- **Embrace the Sensory Overload:** Immerse yourself in the sights, sounds, and smells of the market. The cacophony of vendors calling out their wares, the vibrant colors of fresh produce, and the enticing aroma of local delicacies all contribute to the unique market experience.

- **Respect the Pace:** Unlike the hurried pace of some Western markets, Montenegrin markets have a more relaxed atmosphere. Take your time browsing the stalls, engage with the vendors, and don't be afraid to ask questions (even if your Montenegrin is limited, most vendors understand basic English).
- **Embrace the Bargaining:** Bargaining is an integral part of the market culture in Montenegro. Don't be afraid to negotiate prices! Start with an offer that's lower than the initial asking price and work your way up to a mutually agreeable price. Remember, bargaining is a friendly dance, not a competition. Approach it with a smile and a sense of humor.

Common Bargaining Phrases (with a Montenegrin Twist)

Here are a few basic phrases in Montenegrin to help you navigate the bargaining process:

- **Koja je cijena? (Koy-a ye tsee-ye-na):** How much is this?
- **Previše je skupo (Preh-vee-she ye skoo-po):** It's too expensive.
- **Može biti malo niže? (Mo-zhe bee-tee mah-lo nee-zhe):** Can it be a little lower?
- **Hvala (Hvah-la):** Thank you.
- **Do viđenja (Do vee-dje-nya):** Goodbye (See you again).

Cultural Nuances: Understanding Market Etiquette

While bargaining is expected, keep in mind some cultural nuances:

- **Be Respectful:** Maintain a friendly and respectful demeanor throughout the bargaining process. Don't be aggressive or try to haggle excessively.

- **A Smile Goes a Long Way:** A friendly smile can go a long way in building rapport with vendors. A little Montenegrin goes a long way too – learn a few basic phrases to show your effort and appreciation for their culture.

- **Walk Away if Needed:** Don't feel pressured to buy something you don't want or can't afford. If you can't reach an agreement on a price, politely thank the vendor and move on.

Unique Souvenirs: Bringing Back a Piece of Montenegro

Your Montenegrin market finds should be more than just trinkets. Imagine selecting souvenirs that tell a story, handcrafted treasures that embody the spirit of the country, or local delicacies that bring back memories of delicious meals. Here are some unique souvenir ideas:

- **Handicrafts:** Look for beautiful hand-embroidered tablecloths, traditionally woven baskets, or intricately carved wooden objects. These pieces showcase the skill of local artisans and add a touch of Montenegrin charm to your home.

- **Local Produce:** Indulge in some local delicacies like "Njeguški pršut" (smoked ham), "Pršuta" (prosciutto), or fragrant olive oil. These regional specialties are perfect for gifting or savoring upon your return home.

- **Jewelry:** Montenegro boasts a rich tradition of filigree jewelry making. Look for delicate necklaces, earrings, or bracelets made from silver or gold, each piece a testament to the intricate artistry of local craftspeople.

- **Traditional Clothing:** For a truly unique souvenir, consider purchasing a " kapa," a traditional Montenegrin cap with a red crown. It's a conversation starter and a reminder of your Montenegrin adventure.

- **Local Wines and Rakija:** Montenegro produces some excellent wines and rakija (a strong Balkan brandy). A bottle of local wine or rakija is a perfect way to share a taste of Montenegro with friends and family back home.

The beauty of shopping at local markets lies in finding souvenirs that resonate with your memories. Imagine strolling through the market in Kotor, the salty sea air still clinging to your clothes, and selecting a hand-painted ceramic plate depicting the Bay of Kotor's stunning scenery. Or perhaps you pick up a woven scarf from a village market lay close amidst rolling hills, a reminder of the picturesque landscapes you encountered. These souvenirs become more than just objects; they transform into tangible memories of your Montenegrin adventure.

Supporting Local Artisans

By purchasing from local artisans and small businesses at the markets, you're not just acquiring souvenirs; you're contributing to the preservation of traditional crafts and supporting the local economy. Imagine the satisfaction of knowing your purchase helps sustain the livelihood of skilled artisans and keeps these time-honored traditions alive.

Beyond the Markets: Unique Shopping Experiences

While local markets offer a treasure trove of finds, Montenegro boasts other unique shopping experiences:

- **Family-Run Wineries:** Embark on a wine tasting tour at a family-run winery, learn about local grape varietals, and discover the perfect bottle to take home.

- **Olive Oil Producers:** Visit an olive grove and olive oil producer, witness the traditional harvesting process, and sample some of Montenegro's finest olive oil.

- **Antique Shops:** For the vintage enthusiast, explore antique shops in towns like Kotor or Budva, where you might unearth hidden treasures like old postcards, jewelry, or decorative items.

Shopping in Montenegro is an adventure in itself. From bustling market stalls overflowing with local produce to hidden antique shops brimming with forgotten treasures, each encounter offers a chance to discover something special. So, embrace the art of bargaining, support local artisans, and let your shopping experiences become an extension of your captivating Montenegrin adventure. With a suitcase full of unique souvenirs and a heart brimming with memories, you'll return home with a deeper appreciation for the country's rich culture, warm hospitality, and undeniable charm.

Conclusion

As your Montenegrin adventure draws to a close, a bittersweet feeling washes over you. The turquoise waters beckon one last swim, the cobbled streets whisper tales of history, and the warmth of Montenegrin hospitality lingers in your heart. This captivating country has woven its magic around you, leaving you yearning for more.

Montenegro has unveiled a kaleidoscope of experiences. Imagine the thrill of conquering a mountain peak, the serenity of exploring a hidden cove, or the joy of savoring a delicious meal in a charming village square. You've navigated bustling markets, bargained with friendly vendors, and returned home with unique treasures that tell stories of your adventure.

But Montenegro's magic extends far beyond the sights and experiences. It's the feeling of connection you forge with the land, the warmth of the local people, and the sense of stepping back in time as you explore ancient towns and dramatic landscapes. Montenegro awakens a sense of wonder and a thirst for exploration, leaving an indelible mark on your soul.

As you bid farewell to Montenegro, a promise whispers in your heart – a promise to return. Perhaps you'll conquer the summit of Mount Durmitor next time, delve deeper into the rich history of Cetinje, or discover new hidden coves along the breathtaking coastline. One thing is certain: Montenegro's allure is undeniable, and its magic will beckon you back for another unforgettable adventure.

So, dear reader, pack your bags with a sense of adventure, an open mind, and a camera to capture the memories. Montenegro awaits, ready to captivate your senses and leave you yearning for more. Embark on your journey, discover your own story within this Balkan paradise, and fall in love with Montenegro, just as we all have.

Bonus

Montenegrin Phrasebook

English Phrase	Montenegrin Phrase	Pronunciation
Hello	Zdravo (formal) / Ćao (informal)	ZDRAV-oh (formal) / CHAO (informal)
Goodbye	Doviđenja	Doh-vee-JEH-nyah
Thank you	Hvala	HVA-la
You're welcome	Molim	MO-leem
Please	Molim	MO-leem
Yes	Da	Da
No	Ne	Neh
Excuse me	Izvinite	Iz-vee-NEE-teh
Do you speak English?	Govorite li engleski?	Go-voh-REE-te lee en-GLES-kee
Water	Voda	VOH-da
Beer	Pivo	PEE-voh
Wine	Vino	VEE-no
Coffee	Kava	KAH-va
The bill, please	Račun, molim	RAH-choon, MO-leem
Where is the bathroom?	Gde je toalet?	Gdeh ye twah-LET
How much is this?	Koliko košta ovo?	KOH-lee-koh KOHSH-ta OH-voh
Do you have...?	Imate li...?	ee-MAH-te lee...?
Where is...?	Gde je...?	Gdeh ye...?
Can I get a taxi?	Može li taxi?	MO-zhe lee tahk-SEE
Help!	Pomoć!	PO-mohch
Numbers (1-10)	Jedan, dva, tri, četiri, pet, šest, sedam, osam, devet, deset	YEH-dan, dvah, tree, cheh-tee-ri, pet, shesht, seh-dam, oh-sahm, deh-vet, deh-set
Delicious!	Uk вкусно!	Ookh-oos-no

| Thank you for the meal! | Hvala na ugosćavanju! | HVA-la na oo-goh-chah-vah-nyu |

Printed in Dunstable, United Kingdom

64838015R00077